2005

To Mai, Hugo, + Bori B...

now known

From

Mai's Mum + Dad
&
Josephi Nain + Taid

Vegetarian

Baby & Child

Vegetarian

Baby & Child

Petra Jackson

Quantum Books

A QUANTUM BOOK

This book is produced by
Quantum Publishing Ltd.
6 Blundell Street
London N7 9BH

This edition printed 2002

ISBN 1-86160-577-3

QUMVBC

Printed in China by
Leefung Asco Printers Ltd.

Contents

Introduction

There has never been a more gratifying time to raise your precious baby on a healthy diet without meat. Hardly a week goes by without a report from a scientific source recommending that we should cut back on our consumption of animal produce, and correspondingly increase the amount of fresh fruit, vegetables, whole grains and pulses we eat. Vegetarians have been doing just that for years.

Why be a vegetarian?

The reasons for becoming a vegetarian are as individual and numerous as the vegetarian population, which, according to World statistics, is growing annually in the west by roughly 17%. Becoming more health-conscious is one of the main reasons quoted for embracing vegetarianism; when you consider that most of the animals reared for eating are fed on an alarming cocktail of hormones, antibiotics and other chemicals, whose long-term effects on animals and humans aren't known, it is not surprising that we don't want our children exposed to these unnecessary dangers. Can it be coincidence that childhood disorders, such as eczema, asthma and psoriasis, appear to have increased in parallel with increasingly high levels of meat consumption?

Equally importantly, why should we inflict misery and suffering on animals purely in the name of profit and eating pleasure? Ecologically, there are sound reasons to be a vegetarian. Since the end of the second world war we have destroyed over 40% of the tropical rain forests to lay down grass plains for raising beef cattle. This is madness when you consider that, compared to the huge amount of plant stuff eaten by animals, only 10% ends up on our plates. It makes more sense to forget the cows and eat the plants ourselves.

There are other advantages to raising your child as a vegetarian. A decade or two ago it would have been considered cranky, but, thankfully, the health message is slowly dripping through and a vegetarian diet is now something to aspire to rather than despise.

The time when being a non-meat-eater can become a little tricky is when your children become older; you tend to have less control of their eating habits. Birthday parties used to be the first minefields, with the ubiquitous sausage roll; nowadays, with more mothers working, it may be your child-minder whom you will need to advise of your little one's dietary preferences. The best way to get round this is to find a like-minded carer, or to arrange to provide all your baby's food yourself. At parties and other social events where meat is likely to be served, tell the parents of the party-giver. In these enlightened times it is unlikely that your child will be the only vegetarian in the group.

What is a vegetarian?

Vegetarians fall into three main groups:

Vegans Vegans eat only plant-based foods, and no dairy products, eggs, milk, etc.

Strict Vegetarians Strict vegetarians do not eat any animal, or animal-based product if the animal was killed for the purpose, but they do eat some dairy products, such as eggs, milk and yogurt and rennet-free cheese (labelled vegetarian cheese).

Lacto-vegetarians Lacto-vegetarians simply don't eat dead animals. The lacto-vegetarian diet tends to be unique to the individual: most will eat dairy products, though some will eat only vegetarian cheese, and will certainly not touch lard or gelatine (the gelling agent derived from rendered animal bones). It is towards this latter group that this book is aimed. You may also have heard of people calling themselves "demi-vegetarians", who eat fish and white meat, but this book concentrates on the needs of lacto-vegetarians.

Your child's nutritional requirements

Overleaf are two pages outlining the six essential nutrients required for a healthy human. Here you can discover the role of each nutrient in maintaining the body and the best food sources of each. The recommended daily allowances of each nutrient will vary according to the baby's age and sex. It is important to remember that a growing baby's nutritional needs are as individual as the baby – what may be satisfying for one child might be starvation for another. More simply, the wider the variety of foods your child enjoys, the more certain you can be that he or she is receiving a balanced diet.

To help you judge what is a balanced diet, foods can be classified into five main groups. Aim to give your child at least one serving from each group every day.

Every food provides energy, which is measured in kilocalories (kcal), popularly known as just "calories". As your baby grows, energy requirements dramatically increase. As well as the same balance of nutrients (protein, carbohydrate, fat, vitamins, minerals and dietary fibre) more food is needed to fuel all that growing. Compared with adults, babies have surprisingly high energy needs: 1,900 calories for a woman; 865 for a one-year-old girl rising to 1,545 calories at 4–6 years.

Your baby's appetite will be the best indicator of how much food to give. As with adults, this will vary from day to day, or week to week and, remember, an emerging new tooth or a cold may affect appetite.

Achieving a balanced diet for your baby is easy if you allow at least one serving from each of these five different groups every day.
Group 1
Pulses, beans, lentils, eggs, tofu and nuts
Group 2
Milk, yogurt, cheese and other milk products
Group 3
Cereals, bread, flour, rice and pasta
Group 4
Vegetable fats, oils, margarine and butter
Group 5
Fresh fruit and vegetables

Six essential nutrients for health

Protein

Protein is needed for growth and for healing. Any extra is used as energy. Protein is made up of 12 essential amino-acids. Soya is the only plant-based food that contains all the amino-acids, but cheese and other dairy products do contain them all. Other vegetarian foods – nuts, seeds, grains and pulses – are still good sources of protein but don't contain all the amino-acids.

Fats

Fats are required for energy; fat-stores help the young baby to maintain body heat. Foods that contain fat also include the fat-soluble vitamins, A, D, E and K, which is why it is important that babies drink whole milk (full-fat milk), for at least their first three years.

Carbohydrate

Carbohydrate is the body's main source of energy. It comes in two forms: starches and sugars. There are refined and unrefined versions.

Refined sugars are found in soft drinks, cakes and biscuits; natural sources are fruits, vegetables, and fruit juices. Refined starches are found in white flour, bread, rice and pasta, as well as processed breakfast cereals. Unrefined starches are found in potatoes, pulses and dried beans, whole-grain cereals, bread and flour. In both cases it is the natural, unrefined sources that are the best choice for nutrition and health.

Vitamins

Vitamins are essential for growth and for the healthy maintenance of the body. There are two types: fat-soluble and water-soluble.

Water-soluble vitamins, that is the B group and vitamin C, cannot be stored in the body, so it is important that you feed your baby foods containing these every day. These vitamins are easily dissolved in water and destroyed by heat; so take care, when preparing foods rich in Vitamin C, not to overcook them or to leave them immersed in water for any length of time.

The fat-soluble vitamins are vitamins A, D, E, and K.

It is unusual for children in developed countries to require

vitamin supplements if they eat a balanced diet. However, because vitamins are essential for development of the brain and central nervous system, parents of vegetarian – and more particularly vegan – children should discuss this matter with their doctor or paediatrician.

The primary importance of each vitamin is as follows:

Vitamin A promotes growth, and healthy skin and teeth enamel and good eyesight.
Sources: apricots, whole milk and eggs, carrots, oranges, tomatoes, dark-green vegetables, margarine, lentils.

Vitamin B group, confusingly, covers a large number of different B vitamins. They are necessary aids for digestion, for maintaining a healthy nervous system and for changing food into energy.
Sources: B-group vitamins are found together in many foods, but a vegetarian's main complete source is yeast extract. Other sources include: eggs, wholegrain cereals, bananas, potatoes, nuts and dried beans.

Vitamin C is essential for growth and healing and it must be present if the body is to absorb iron properly.
Sources: this vitamin is found in all fruit and vegetables; the best sources are citrus fruit, kiwi fruit, blackcurrants, cranberries, strawberries, tomatoes, green vegetables, peppers, potatoes, cauliflower.

Vitamin D works with calcium to create healthy bones and teeth.
Sources: oils, eggs, margarine.

Vitamin E is necessary for the composition of body cells. It also helps to maintain and create new red blood cells.
Sources: vegetable oils, margarine, nuts.

Vitamin K aids blood-clotting and helps maintain the skeleton.
Sources: wholegrain cereals, most vegetables.

Minerals

Calcium and iron are the two essential minerals. Calcium is needed for strong bones and teeth; iron for healthy blood cells and muscle growth. Calcium-rich foods are milk and cheese, dried fruit, bread, flour, pulses and some green vegetables. Iron is mainly found in egg-yolks, whole-grain cereals, green leafy vegetables and chocolate.

Water

Babies are more at risk from dehydrating than adults. It is vital that you maintain your baby's fluid levels with regular drinks. In the first weeks of life, most babies, particularly those who are breast-fed, need no more than their regular feeds. However, in hot weather, or when travelling, a supply of cooled, freshly boiled water will help quench your baby's thirst.

Food allergies

The main point to remember on this subject is that food allergies are very rare. Unless there is a family history of food allergies, there is no reason to suppose your baby will suffer. Moreover, as babies' immune systems are not fully matured, a food that causes a reaction in one month may prove harmless a month or two later. If you introduce foods one at a time you will reduce the risk of a reaction, and can identify the culprit easily, if there is a reaction.

The main symptoms of an allergic reaction are:

- vomiting (some babies vomit more than others anyway, but you can probably tell if vomiting is more serious than usual);
- vomiting coupled with diarrhoea;
- diarrhoea;
- rash (from pale pink to deeper coloured blotches);
- swelling;
- continual crying (again, you can probably judge if your baby is crying more than usual);
- baby draws its knees up and cries.

If you believe your baby has an allergy, or are at all worried about feeding or are in any doubt of your child's well-being, never feel afraid to consult your doctor. Babies can fall ill very quickly, and vomiting and diarrhoea will dehydrate them rapidly, so always call in the experts.

Always listen to and follow the expert advice you get from your doctor, paediatrician or dietitian. They will know what is best. Don't try to diagnose or treat the baby yourself.

Common food allergies

Gluten Gluten is the protein found in wheat, barley, oats and rye. Sensitivity to gluten can lead to coeliac disease, which is why doctors recommend that all babies follow a gluten-free diet in the first year.

Cow's milk protein A baby sensitive to cow's milk protein will be prescribed a modified, soya-based milk. Breast-feeding mothers of babies with this sensitivity should perhaps cut down on their dairy intake, if advised by a doctor, as the protein they eat can be transferred to the baby.

Lactose intolerance Lactose is a milk sugar. Infants who suffer from an intolerance to it do not have an allergy in the true sense: rather, they lack the enzyme lactase, which is needed for breaking down lactose into simple sugars. Moreover, some children who are lactose-intolerant can happily eat other dairy products.

Eggs A very few babies are allergic to eggs. In addition, though not an allergy, the problem of salmonella contamination in raw or undercooked eggs needs to be considered. Guidelines are that you can give hard-cooked egg-yolks after eight months and similarly cooked egg-whites and whole eggs after a year.

Planning and freezing meals

You will see that the chapters in this book are divided by age group, starting from when you first start to wean your baby through to the toddler and then school age. At the end of each chapter there is a four-week menu planner, to help you choose your child's meals. There are quite a few choices, but, in reality, you will most frequently repeat the recipes your child enjoys most. This is where your freezer will come in handy. By the age of 9–10 months your baby will probably be eating the same meals as the family. An easy and efficient way to feed them is to prepare and freeze baby-size portions of whatever you are cooking. Each recipe states whether it is suitable for freezing. You may like to prepare and freeze double batches of certain foods, particularly cookies, bread and pastry cases.

Freezing baby foods

When you are preparing purees for your baby, it makes sense to make more than you need and freeze the remainder. If you do this every time you cook, you'll save yourself a lot of time and work. You'll soon build up a stock of meals for when time is short, leaving you more time to enjoy being with your child.

You will need a freezer that can freeze food to −18°C and your containers must be sterile. In the early days, when you need only a small quantity, ice-cube trays are ideal. When you need larger helpings, use rigid, plastic, sealable freezer containers or freezerproof dishes. When your baby is around eight months old, and crawling, you no longer need to sterilize the dishes.

Three steps to success

1 Sterilize the ice-cube trays by whichever method you normally use (see page 20) and switch your freezer to fast-freeze an hour before you need it.

2 Cook and purée the food as described in the recipe. Cover it with a clean tea towel, or non-PVC cling film, but do not allow these to touch the food. Leave in a cool place (not the fridge) until completely cold. Using a sterilized spoon, divide the purée between the ice-cube tray sections and freeze until hard (about two hours).

3 Reset the freezer to normal. Release the frozen cubes into new freezer bags. Seal and label the bags and keep them in the freezer for up to a month. Thaw individual portions in a loosely covered, sterilized dish. Reheat the food thoroughly in a saucepan of simmering water and let it cool to a suitable temperature before serving.

Only freeze freshly prepared foods; *never* freeze uneaten portions.

The vegetarian kitchen and larder

When you have a family to feed, you need to organise yourself, which means keeping a store of basic ingredients. If you have both a fridge and a freezing cabinet of a reasonable size, you shouldn't have to go shopping for fresh foods every day.

Buying food for a young baby is easy, because they eat only small quantities of a limited number of foods, but, as time goes on, you will need to extend your storecup board. Here is a list of the essentials for a growing family. Use it as a guide the next time you go shopping. Bear in mind that some items will only be available in season; the vegetarian diet makes the most of the pleasures of choosing food that is at its very best and freshest at the time you buy it.

Fresh foods

It is better to give your baby fresh rather than processed foods. Fruit and vegetables are the obvious first candidates. Choose good-quality items. But be penny-wise with your purchases too; remember that fresh produce spoils and deteriorates fast, so you may find it more suitable to shop at a local greengrocer or market, where you can buy little and often.

Fruits Puréed apple and mashed banana are probably the first fruit your baby will enjoy. Apples are a good source of vitamin C, while bananas are rich in potassium and fibre.

Dried foods

These can be classified into four main groups and include long-life storecupboard basics, such as flour, rice and cereals. These are items that you can add to your larder on each shopping trip. Buying just one item from each group will ensure your storecupboard is well stocked. Frozen foods are another kind of storecupboard item, and will enable you to take advantage of fresh seasonal purchases.

Starches The sources of these, such as bread, pasta, rice and so on, add bulk as well as protein and minerals to a baby's diet. Wholemeal varieties have a higher nutritional value.

Vegetables With so many different vegetables to choose from, a meat-free diet need never be boring. Potatoes and other root vegetables are rich in vitamins A and C and cook to a splendid purée, perfect for babies' first tastes.

Dairy Children will benefit from this concentrated source of protein, calcium, energy in the form of fats, as well as the fat-soluble vitamins D and E. Cartons of fruit yogurt make great instant puddings.

Miscellaneous There is an enormous variety of fresh fruit juice in the shops: diluted for babies, they make great thirst-quenchers.

Groceries These form the backbone of any storecupboard and comprise the usual essentials, such as dried fruits, nuts, seeds, honey, sugar, herbs and spices. Ingredients like these can enhance even the most mundane dishes. Keep in sealed containers away from direct light.

Cans and Condiments Items such as canned pulses and beans, tomatoes, and soft fruits along with prepared sauces, oils and vinegar are essential storecupboard items. Their long shelf life means that shopping for these can be done in bulk, often saving you time and money.

CHAPTER 1

Babies

4 - 8 MONTHS

For the first six months of your baby's life, milk will be the principal nourishment. Breast milk contains all the six essential nutrients your baby needs (see Six Essential Nutrients for Health, page 10), while formula milk, which can be based on cow's or soya milk, will be ready-fortified with vitamins and minerals.

Your guide to weaning

When to start?

There are no hard and fast rules about when you should begin introducing your baby to solid foods. But remember that a baby's system is not capable of digesting anything other than milk in its first weeks of life, and that starting on solids too soon may result in food intolerance or allergies later.

Opinions on timing differ: some say you should start solids when the baby is of a certain weight, around 7.25 kg (16 lb), or at 20 weeks old. Generally, your baby will let you know when it is time. Good indications are if the baby become restless and unsettled during the night, if the intervals between each feed shorten over a prolonged period or the baby starts putting a hand (or anything else within reach) into its mouth.

What should it be?

Nature must be on the vegetarian side, because, to begin with, all babies are vegetarian. The first foods to offer are those that can be ground down to a pulp, making vegetables and fruit the ideal candidates, but there is no reason not to try cereal.

Start by offering one food only, such as puréed potato or apple. Give this for a couple of days before trying something new. In this way, if your baby does have an adverse reaction, you will know the likely culprit. Then work up to combining foods. During this time, remember not to cut down on milk feeds.

How much to give?

You will probably find that your baby will only take in about a teaspoon or two of purée at the beginning. Allow about 15 ml (1 tablespoon), or 1 ice-cube portion taken from an ice-cube tray (see page 13).

One lump or two?

It is mainly with their mouths that babies find out about the world: their chief experience is oral and so it naturally follows that the texture of food is very important to them. At the beginning, purées should be very soft and wet, almost liquid. You will probably have to thin some of them with baby milk, diluted fruit juice or freshly boiled water. As your baby gets used to thicker textures, you can reduce the amount of liquid. Mashing, grating or finely chopping food encourages chewing as the baby gets older and starts teething. Food can be cooked more lightly, fruit can be offered raw, and, after about eight months, your baby can be given rice cakes, bread, raw carrots and so on, to hold and suck.

What to use?

There is no need to buy your baby a special dinner service! Tiny portions need only tiny feeding bowls, so any small dishes that can be sterilized will be fine; I suggest starting off using the top of a feeding bottle. Progress to a ramekin dish. Try to use the same style of spoon for every food: babies learn most about their world through their mouths, and it is best to keep to a familiar object. Shallow, plastic weaning spoons are best. Look for entertainingly shaped ones such as aeroplanes or trains. Accompanied by the right sound effects, these can liven up mealtimes and encourage eating.

For an older baby, jolly coloured melamine bowls and dishes can help make meal times more fun. Again, it's not necessary to have a whole range, as babies often like to have their favourite dish all the time. Two bowls, plates and dishes should be ample. Spoons often have a habit of disappearing, however, so it's a good idea to start off with at least six.

How to start?

Make up the feed in readiness. It is a good idea to have it at the same temperature as you would baby milk, but as long as it is not too hot it shouldn't matter.

Put the feed into a small, sterilized dish.

Lunch time is usually a good time to begin. Give your baby a partial milk feed first to satisfy immediate hunger. A screaming, hungry baby will not be receptive to new ideas!

Hold your baby in the normal feeding position. Use a bib to catch spills and you may find it a good idea to cover yourself too. Choose a small, shallow plastic spoon and away you go.

A baby's first dinner service and cutlery set needn't be extensive; babies prefer familiar objects, so a set of each should be sufficient. Opt for those made from unbreakable melamine, available in lots of designs.

Establishing a routine

Try to feed your baby at the same time every day. Put everything that you need to hand before you start. Tying the bib round your baby's neck is a sure signal that it's feeding time. Babies of six months or more, who are able to sit in a high chair, can be given an empty bowl and spoon to play with while you prepare their meals. They sometimes like a companion to share mealtimes – try a favourite teddy or soft toy. (Protect these from spills with a bib of their own.) Babies like to exert their independence from a startlingly early age, so as soon as they start grabbing for the spoon, let them try to hold it themselves. Trying to copy you is common – let your baby try to feed you or teddy and don't worry about the mess. Protect the floor with newspaper or a binliner that you can just scoop up and discard afterwards.

What if you have problems?

Don't be anxious or hurt if your baby won't eat at first. Leave it and try again the next day, or in a couple of days' time. In the very early days, milk will still be the main form of nourishment for your baby. The aim of feeding solids, at first, is to encourage the use of the muscles of the mouth, and co-ordination of the tongue and throat, by swallowing thicker-textured substances, and to begin introducing your baby to the idea of mealtimes. The best way to show them that eating can be enjoyable is to let them join in family mealtimes as soon as possible; if necessary, bring forward your family meal, so the baby can be part of it.

If you do have several refusals, try going straight to a fairly wet solid feed rather than starting with a milk feed to take the edge off the baby's appetite. Offer milk afterwards. The main thing is to avoid making a fuss and stay relaxed yourself. You can't bribe a young baby to eat: they don't understand.

For some reason, you can never have enough bibs. Choose the soft, absorbent, brightly coloured cotton terry-towelling type.

Preparing food for your baby

Equipment

In the beginning you don't need elaborate food-preparation equipment. As your baby is only eating tiny quantities, a sterilized sieve and spoon are all that is required to purée food. When your baby starts to eat more, it may be worth buying a blender or food processor. Hand-held blenders are particularly good, because they can cope with varying amounts of food and will prove useful for some time to come. However when using a blender or food processor you will still have to sieve some foods to get rid of any tough fibres or pips.

A steamer is also a worthwhile investment. Choose a multi-tiered type, which will allow you to cook several different dishes at the same time. Initially, you can get by with a heatproof sieve covered with a lid or foil and set over a pan of simmering water.

Whisks and blenders reduce the effort of preparing liquidized food.

Cooking

Young babies need almost all their foods to be cooked, if they are to digest them easily. By far the best cooking method is steaming, but boiling, stewing or baking can all be used.

Wash the fruit or vegetable of your choice, peel, stone or de-seed it as appropriate, and then chop it in evenly sized pieces. Cook the fruit and vegetable in a steamer. Or place the food in a saucepan and just cover it with cold water; bring the water to the boil and simmer for about 10 minutes, or as stated in the recipe.

Sterilizing

Hygiene is of the utmost importance. All bottles, feeding cups, spoons and so on should be washed and sterilized. Once your baby is mobile, and starts to investigate the world via what it can put in its mouth, you can relax a bit about sterilizing the feeding things. Milk bottles and teats should still be sterilized for up to a year, however.

Boiling Utensils should be completely immersed in boiling water for 5 minutes. Remove them with tongs and let them dry quickly in the air.

Steaming A cabinet specifically designed to take baby bottles, teats and other utensils is the best method for steaming. A timer and thermostat incorporated in the machine ensures that the correct time and temperature for sterilizing is set.

Sterilizing fluid/tablets You can buy commercial fluid or compressed tablets which are dissolved in water. You need a purpose-made water tank or a covered plastic container.

Menu planner
Your four-week baby mealtime guide

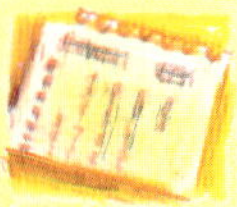	 Early morning	 Late morning	 Lunch	 Afternoon	 Tea	 Bedtime
Week 1						
Days 1–7	milk	milk	puréed vegetable	milk	puréed fruit	milk
Week 2						
Same as week 1						
Week 3						
Days 1 & 2	milk	milk	Vegetable Duo	milk	Orchard Purée	milk
Days 3 & 4	milk	milk	Vegetable Trio	milk	Banana Rice	milk
Days 5 & 6	milk	milk	Risotto	milk	Fruit Cream	milk
Day 7	milk & banana	milk	Baked Sweet Potato	milk	Peach Cake	milk
Week 4						
Day 1	milk & banana	milk	Baked Pumpkin with Orange	milk	Cauliflower Fluff	milk
Day 2	milk & banana	milk	Cream of Vegetables; Dried-Fruit Compote	milk	Tropical Dream	milk
Day 3	milk & pear	milk	Poached Parsley Mushrooms	milk	Teatime Tomatoes and Tofu	milk
Day 4	milk & pear	milk	Lentil and Tomato Medley; Passion Pudding	milk	Pom-Poms	milk
Day 5	milk & apple	milk	Baked Beets and Potato; Rice Pudding	milk	Fruit Cream	milk
Day 6	milk & apple	milk	Vegetable Quartet; Apricot Condé	milk	Fruit Cream	milk
Day 7	milk & peach	milk	Risotto; Dutch Apples	milk	Teeny Tahini	milk

Puréeing
Making purées couldn't be simpler. Drain the cooked fruit or vegetable and allow it to cool for a few minutes. Push it through a sieve or blend it until it is completely smooth. Add a little of the cooking water, freshly boiled water or baby milk to adjust the consistency.

Use this menu planner (above) as a guide, but if your baby prefers one dish to another, offer this on several occasions. Don't make lots of work for yourself planning new meals every day. At teatime offer a separate drink: try diluted fruit juice or cooled, freshly boiled water.

LUNCHES

A variety of easy-to-prepare nutritious savoury purées to get your baby started on the right track. Don't be too concerned if your baby doesn't appear interested at first. Babies have a naturally sweet tooth (breast milk is very sweet) and new flavours take getting used to.

MAKES: *5 portions*
PREPARATION TIME: *10 minutes*
COOKING TIME: *15 minutes*
FREEZING: *recommended*

INGREDIENTS
115 g (4 oz) potato, peeled and cut in small cubes
baby milk

HINTS AND TIPS

If you are baking potatoes for the family, bake one for your baby too. Preheat the oven to Gas Mark 6/ 200°C/400°F. Scrub the potatoes well and prick them all over. Bake for 1 hour. Halve the potatoes, scrape out the flesh with a clean teaspoon and then continue from step 3, above.

Potato purée

Puréed potatoes are a good choice of food to start your baby eating solids. They contain quite a lot of vitamin C and provide an excellent bland base that you can combine with other flavours as your baby becomes used to a wider range.

1 Put the potato cubes in a small saucepan and pour in enough cold water just to cover them.
2 Bring the water to the boil, cover the pan and simmer for 10–15 minutes, or until the potatoes are tender. Drain well.
3 Mash the potatoes with enough baby milk to give a smooth paste. Press the paste through a sterilized sieve. Add more baby milk if necessary to obtain a thick, slightly runny consistency.

Vegetable duos

Other root vegetables, such as carrot, swede and parsnip, can be easy partners for potatoes. They can be prepared and cooked together, so saving you time and effort.

MAKES: *10 portions*
PREPARATION TIME: *10 minutes*
COOKING TIME: *15 minutes*
FREEZING: *recommended*

INGREDIENTS
115 g (4 oz) potato, peeled and cut in small cubes
115 g (4 oz) carrot, parsnip or swede, peeled and cut in small cubes
baby milk

1 Put the cubed vegetables in a small saucepan and pour in enough water just to cover them. Bring the water to the boil, cover the pan and simmer for 10–15 minutes, or until the vegetables are tender. Drain well.
2 Mash the vegetables with baby milk to a smooth paste. Press the paste through a sterilized sieve and add more baby milk if necessary, to obtain a thick, slightly runny consistency.

Vegetable trio

Combine the starchy root vegetable with tomatoes for a lighter alternative. Once skinned and de-seeded, tomatoes are easily digested; and although they contain a lot of water they are also a good source of vitamins A and C.

MAKES: *10 portions*
PREPARATION TIME: *15 minutes*
COOKING TIME: *15 minutes*
FREEZING: *recommended*

INGREDIENTS
115 g (4 oz) potato, peeled and cut in small cubes
115 g (4 oz) carrot, peeled and cut in small cubes
1 firm, ripe tomato
baby milk

1 Put the cubed vegetables in a small saucepan. Pour in enough water just to cover them.
2 Bring the water to the boil, cover the pan and simmer for 10–15 minutes, or until the vegetables are tender.
3 Meanwhile, put the tomato into a small bowl and pour over enough boiling water to cover it. Leave for 30 seconds. Drain and rinse under cold running water and carefully rub away the skin.
4 Drain the potato and carrot when they are cooked. Halve the tomato, remove the core and scoop out all the seeds. Chop the flesh very finely and then mash it with the cooked vegetables and baby milk to a smooth paste. Press the paste through a sterilized sieve, adding more milk if necessary, to obtain a slightly runny paste.

Vegetable quartet

MAKES: *12 portions*
PREPARATION TIME: *15 minutes*
COOKING TIME: *20 minutes*
FREEZING: *recommended*

INGREDIENTS
60 g (2 oz) white part of leek
115 g (4 oz) potato, peeled
115 g (4 oz) swede, peeled
1 firm, ripe tomato, skinned and de-seeded
300 ml (½ pint) vegetable stock (see page 138)

As feeding progresses, combine new flavours with those that your baby has already become familiar with. Leeks have a sweeter, milder flavour than onions; they can be introduced when your baby is about 5 months old.

1 Carefully wash the leek to remove all soil and then trim it and slice it finely. Cut the potato and swede in small cubes. Put all the prepared vegetables in a small saucepan and add the stock.
2 Bring the stock to the boil, cover the pan and simmer for 15–20 minutes, or until the vegetables are tender. Purée the vegetables with the stock until smooth. Allow to cool slightly before serving.

Cream of vegetables

MAKES: *about 12 portions*
PREPARATION TIME: *20 minutes*
COOKING TIME: *varies according to vegetable used*
FREEZING: *not recommended*

INGREDIENTS
115 g (4 oz) courgette, French beans, broccoli, or spinach
half a vegetarian, gluten-, salt- and sugar-free rusk
about 175 ml (6 fl oz) baby milk
10–15 ml (2–3 teaspoons) freshly boiled water

In this recipe, vegetables are combined with a small salt- and sugar-free rusk and baby milk to provide a more substantial purée than one using just vegetables. This is particularly suitable for the more watery vegetables. As your baby gets older, make the cream thicker by reducing the amount of liquid you add at the end of step 4.

1 Prepare your vegetable: trim and slice courgette or beans; divide broccoli into small florets; remove any tough stalks from spinach. Rinse well and drain.
2 Steam the vegetable for 10–15 minutes (5–10 minutes for spinach), or until tender.
3 Meanwhile, crumble the rusk into a small dish and warm the baby milk. Mix together to form a smooth paste.
4 Purée the vegetable with the freshly boiled water until smooth. Sieve if necessary. Stir into the milk mixture and mix with more baby milk or boiled water to obtain a smooth, thick runny consistency.

HINTS AND TIPS

A similar cream can be prepared using 10–15 ml (2–3 teaspoons) of a commercial baby rice in place of the rusk. Check the packet for ingredients and instructions.

Baked sweet potato

MAKES: *6 portions*
PREPARATION TIME: *15 minutes*
COOKING TIME: *1 hour*
FREEZING: *recommended*

Sweet potatoes have a delicious flavour that babies love. They are a great source of carbohydrate, vitamins and minerals and can be baked or boiled. Parsnip is an excellent partner for sweet potato.

INGREDIENTS
180 g (6 oz) sweet potato, scrubbed
115 g (4 oz) parsnip, trimmed and peeled
baby milk
a tiny pinch of ground coriander

1 Preheat the oven to Gas Mark 6/200°C/400°F. Cook the vegetables on a baking sheet for about 1 hour or until tender.
2 Halve the sweet potato and, using a teaspoon, scoop out the flesh and put it in a bowl, with the parsnip.
3 Mash with baby milk until soft and smooth. Press through a sieve if necessary and then stir in the coriander.

Baked pumpkin with orange

MAKES: *6 portions*
PREPARATION TIME: *15 minutes*
COOKING TIME: *1½ hours*
FREEZING: *recommended*

A classic combination of flavours, which can be adapted to suit your baby's taste. If possible, use a freshly squeezed orange for the maximum flavour and nutritional benefit.

INGREDIENTS
180 g (6 oz) fresh pumpkin, skinned and de-seeded
1 small orange, squeezed
15 g (½ oz) soya margarine
a pinch of light muscovado sugar

1 Preheat the oven to Gas Mark 5/190°C/375°F. Lightly oil an 18 cm (7-inch) square of foil. Put the pumpkin in the centre of the foil and lift up each corner to form a cup. Pour the orange juice over the pumpkin and dot with the margarine. Sprinkle with sugar.
2 Twist the corners of foil to seal the parcel and then set it on a baking sheet. Cook for 1½ hours, or until the pumpkin is tender.
3 Scoop out the flesh and purée it with the cooking juices until smooth. Allow to cool a little, if necessary, before serving.

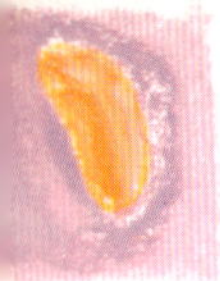

Four-season risottos

EACH RECIPE MAKES: *12 portions*
PREPARATION TIME: *up to 20 minutes*
COOKING TIME: *up to 20 minutes*
FREEZING: *not recommended*

INGREDIENTS
FOR ALL THE RISOTTOS:
30 g (1 oz) unsalted cooked white rice
Baby milk
FOR THE SPRING RISOTTO:
60 g (2 oz) each young carrots and new potatoes, trimmed, peeled and roughly chopped
115 g (4 oz) fresh young spinach leaves, washed and roughly shredded
FOR THE SUMMER RISOTTO:
60 g (2 oz) each courgette and sweet red pepper
1 firm ripe tomato, skinned and de-seeded
FOR THE AUTUMN RISOTTO:
60 g (2 oz) each cauliflower florets, okra and potato
FOR THE WINTER RISOTTO:
60 g (2 oz) each swede, turnip and parsnip, trimmed, peeled and cubed

As the name suggests, this recipe uses seasonal vegetables to provide your baby with the best of the crop. Fresh young spring vegetables, sun-ripened summer crops, autumn brassicas and winter roots provide varying amounts of vitamins A, B, and C, calcium and iron.

1 For the spring risotto, cook the carrot and potato in boiling water for 15 minutes, or until tender. Add the spinach to the water 3 minutes before the end of the cooking time. Drain well.

For the summer risotto, trim the courgette and chop it roughly. Peel the pepper and remove any seeds and fibrous parts. Chop it roughly with the tomato. Steam the vegetables for 10 minutes or until tender.

For the autumn risotto, trim the okra and peel the potato. Cook with the cauliflower in boiling water for 15 minutes, or until tender. Drain well.

For the winter risotto, cook the vegetables in boiling water for 20 minutes, or until tender. Drain well.

2 Purée the vegetables with the rice and enough milk to give a smooth, soft consistency. Push through a sterilized sieve, if necessary.

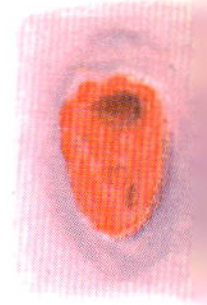

Lentil and tomato medley

Lentils are a good source of protein, but should only be combined with vegetables in small proportions for very young babies.

1 Put the lentils in a saucepan and pour in enough cold water to cover by about 1 cm (½ inch). Bring to the boil, skim any froth from the surface and simmer for 5 minutes. Drain and return to pan.
2 Roughly chop the tomatoes and add them to the lentils, with the tomato juice. Bring to the boil, cover and simmer gently for 25–30 minutes, stirring frequently, until the lentils are very soft. Sieve before serving, and allow to cool a little, if necessary.

MAKES: *6 portions*
PREPARATION TIME: *25 minutes*
COOKING TIME: *35 minutes*
FREEZING: *not recommended*

INGREDIENTS
30 ml (2 tablespoons) red lentils
4 firm, ripe tomatoes, skinned and de-seeded
115 ml (4 fl oz) tomato juice

Poached parsley mushrooms

Choose fresh, open-cup mushrooms and ensure they are wiped thoroughly before poaching them. There is no need to wash or peel mushrooms as long as trapped dirt is carefully wiped away.

1 Poach the mushrooms with the parsley in the baby milk over a low heat for 10–15 minutes, or until tender. Take care that the milk doesn't catch on the base of the pan.
2 Purée to a smooth, soft consistency. Add more milk and allow to cool a little, if necessary.

MAKES: *4 portions*
PREPARATION TIME: *10 minutes*
COOKING TIME: *15 minutes*
FREEZING: *not recommended*

INGREDIENTS
115 g (4 oz) mushrooms, stalks removed, sliced
15 ml (1 tablespoon) chopped fresh parsley
about 115 ml (4 fl oz) baby milk

Baked beets and potato

Beetroot makes a colourful meal and provides a fair amount of vitamin B as well as calcium. Buy raw beetroot rather than ready-cooked ones, because the latter are often soaked in brine.

1 Preheat the oven to Gas Mark 3/160°C/325°F. Remove any whiskery threads from the beetroot; don't pierce the skin, or it will leak during cooking. Place the vegetables in a dish and cover with foil.
2 Cook for 2 hours, or until the vegetables are tender and the beetroot skin will rub away easily.
3 Halve the potato and scoop out the flesh. Purée it with the beetroot and baby milk.

MAKES: *6 portions*
PREPARATION TIME: *10 minutes*
COOKING TIME: *2 hours*
FREEZING: *not recommended*

INGREDIENTS
115 g (4 oz) baby beetroot
180 g (6 oz) potato, scrubbed and pricked
baby milk

TEA

More easy-to-prepare purées, both sweet and savoury, to tempt your baby with. Try to balance the combination of foods you offer your baby in one day. If your baby has had a fairly robust lunch, offer a light fruit purée at teatime. See the suggested menu on page 21 as a guide.

Three-fruit purée

MAKES: *6 portions*
PREPARATION TIME: *15 minutes*
COOKING TIME: *5 minutes*
FREEZING: *not recommended*

INGREDIENTS
2 eating apples, peeled, cored and chopped
1 dessert pear, peeled, cored and chopped
1 ripe plum, skinned and stoned
30 ml (2 tablespoons) apple juice

At the height of their season (early–mid September), plums will be at their sweetest. For young babies they may have a purging effect, so offer only a little, mixed with other fruits. Skin the plum in the same way as you would a tomato.

1 Put the apple and pear into a saucepan with the apple juice and 30 ml (2 tablespoons) water. Bring to the boil.
2 Add the plum and simmer gently for 5 minutes, or until softened. Purée until smooth. Adjust the consistency with freshly boiled water and allow to cool before serving.

Orchard purée

MAKES: *4 portions*
PREPARATION TIME: *15 minutes*
COOKING TIME: *10 minutes*
FREEZING: *recommended*

Puréed apples and pears are ideal fruit for babies; on first taste they may be a little tart, however. If your baby isn't tempted, try combining orchard fruit with sweeter fruit such as mashed banana or, when in season, fresh plums (see Three Fruit Purée, opposite).

INGREDIENTS

1 medium-size eating apple, peeled, cored and chopped
1 medium-size dessert pear, peeled, cored and chopped
30 ml (2 tablespoons) pure apple juice

1 Put the fruit and apple juice in a small saucepan with 30 ml (2 tablespoons) water. Bring to the boil.
2 Cook over a medium heat for 10 minutes, stirring occasionally, until the fruit is tender. Cool slightly and then purée the fruit. Adjust the consistency with freshly boiled water.

Teatime tomatoes and tofu

MAKES: *1 portion*
PREPARATION TIME: *10 minutes*
COOKING TIME: *20 minutes*
FREEZING: *not recommended*

Tofu is protein-packed and incredibly bland in flavour. Make sure you buy fresh or silken tofu, rather than the smoked or flavoured kind.

INGREDIENTS

60 g (2 oz) tofu
1 firm, ripe tomato, skinned, deseeded and roughly chopped
baby milk

1 Preheat the oven to Gas Mark 4/180°C/350°F. Lightly grease a 150 ml (¼ pint) ramekin dish with sunflower oil.
2 Drain the tofu and purée it with the tomato and about 10 ml (2 teaspoons) of baby milk, until smooth. Spoon into the ramekin and cook for 15–20 minutes until risen and set.
3 Spoon into a cold dish and allow to cool for a few minutes before serving.

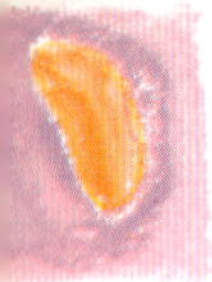

MAKES: *4 portions*
PREPARATION TIME: *10 minutes*
COOKING TIME: *1 hour*
FREEZING: *recommended*

INGREDIENTS
180 g (6 oz) potato, scrubbed
1 eating apple, cored
baby milk

Pom-poms

Apple and potato is an unusual combination it's true, but with an appealing texture and mild flavour, and lots of vitamins B and C, it's sure to be a winner.

1 Preheat the oven to Gas Mark 6/200°C/400°F. Prick the potato Wrap the apple loosely in foil. Bake both for 1 hour or until tender.
2 Halve the potato. Using a teaspoon, scoop out the flesh from the potato and apple and purée it with baby milk. Allow to cool a little, if necessary, before serving.

MAKES: *1 portion*
PREPARATION TIME: *5 minutes*
FREEZING: *not recommended*

INGREDIENTS
½ small, ripe avocado
⅛ teaspoon unsalted tahini paste
baby milk, if necessary

Teeny tahini

Tahini is a paste made from sesame seeds which is used widely in oriental and African recipes. Combined with avocado, it provides huge helpings of unsaturated fat and is a rich source of vitamins B and E.

Remove the stone from the avocado, and, using a teaspoon, scoop out the flesh. Purée it with the tahini paste until smooth. Adjust the consistency with freshly boiled water or baby milk if necessary.

MAKES: *4 portions*
PREPARATION TIME: *15 minutes*
COOKING TIME: *15 minutes*
FREEZING: *not recommended*

INGREDIENTS
115 g (4 oz) cauliflower florets
30 ml (2 tablespoons) fine soya meal
Baby milk or freshly boiled water

Cauliflower fluff

The presence of soya boosts the protein in this teatime savoury. Cauliflower can be a bit strongly flavoured for young babies, so it would be wise to offer this when solid feeding has become more established.

1 Steam the cauliflower florets for 10 minutes, or until tender. Purée them with the soya meal and baby milk or water until smooth.
2 Spoon the mixture into a small saucepan and stir it over a medium heat for 5 minutes, until slightly thickened. Adjust the consistency with more baby milk or freshly boiled water.

Banana rice

Although it's a refined product, commercial baby rice cereal is a great standby. Choose an unflavoured variety and combine it with fruit purées to create your baby's favourite.

MAKES: *1 portion*
PREPARATION TIME: *5 minutes*
FREEZING: *not recommended*

INGREDIENTS
15 ml (1 tablespoon) baby rice cereal
baby milk
½ banana

Make up the baby rice cereal with baby milk or water as directed on the packet. Peel and mash the banana until smooth and then stir in the baby rice cereal. Mix them together thoroughly.

Banana buddies

Bananas, like potatoes, are an ideal base for a number of purées. Alone, they are the perfect convenience food, requiring little preparation and no cooking.

MAKES: *1–2 portions*
PREPARATION TIME: *5 minutes*

INGREDIENTS
½ banana, peeled
1 canned apricot, peach or pear half in natural juice
15 ml (1 tablespoon) of juice from the can

Mash the banana until smooth. Purée the fruit with the juice from the can. Mix into the banana.

HINTS AND TIPS

Other banana buddies can include puréed fresh apple, kiwi fruit, and mango and soaked dried apricots and mango. Make only enough to use at one time, because bananas turn black if kept for any length of time once peeled.

MAKES: *6 portions*
PREPARATION TIME: *10 minutes*
COOKING TIME: *5 minutes*
FREEZING: *not recommended*

INGREDIENTS
1 fresh kiwi fruit, peach or apricot
30 ml (2 tablespoons) unflavoured baby rice cereal
baby milk or freshly boiled water

Fruit creams

Like the recipe for Cream of Vegetables (page 24), this is suited to the more watery fruit, such as kiwi fruit, peaches or apricots. Use unflavoured baby rice.

1 Peel the fruit and remove the stone or seeds as appropriate. Chop the flesh roughly and poach it in 15 ml (1 tablespoon) of water for 5 minutes, until tender.
2 Mix the baby rice cereal with the baby milk or water as directed on the packet. Mix the rice into the fruit and then purée until smooth. Adjust the consistency with more baby milk or freshly boiled water.

Rice pudding

An easy favourite: use flaked rice for quickness and serve with a fruit purée or mashed banana for added sweetness.

MAKES: *2 portions*
PREPARATION TIME: *2 minutes*
COOKING TIME: *10 minutes*
FREEZING: *not recommended*

INGREDIENTS
15 ml (1 tablespoon) flaked rice
150 ml (¼ pint) baby milk

1 Mix the rice and milk together in a small saucepan. Stir over a low heat for 5 minutes or until the mixture thickens and begins to boil.
2 Simmer for 5 minutes, stirring frequently. Allow to cool for a few minutes before feeding this to your baby.

Tropical dream

The custard apple contributes to the soft creamy texture of this recipe, but, like the banana, it blackens on keeping – so prepare this just before you need it.

MAKES: *2 portions*
PREPARATION TIME: *10 minutes*
COOKING TIME: *5 minutes*
FREEZING: *not recommended*

INGREDIENTS
½ ripe mango, peeled and roughly chopped
½ banana
1 small custard apple

1 Poach the mango for 5 minutes with 15 ml (1 tablespoon) water for 5 minutes, or until tender. Purée until smooth.
2 Mash the banana. Halve the custard apple and, using a teaspoon, scoop out the flesh. Mix with the mango and banana and then purée until smooth.

Peach cake

Unsalted rice cakes may not look appealing, but they combine beautifully with soft fruit purées to create new textures and tastes for your baby to try.

MAKES: *4 portions*
PREPARATION TIME: *5 minutes*
FREEZING: *not recommended*

INGREDIENTS
1 unsalted rice cake
about 30 ml (2 tablespoons) peach juice from the can
1 canned peach in natural juice

1 Soak the rice cake in the peach juice until soft. Purée it with the peach until smooth.
2 Adjust the consistency with more juice or freshly boiled water.

PUDDINGS

Babies do not necessarily have to have a two-course meal on every occasion, but it is nice to be able to offer your baby a variety of tastes and textures. Included here are a number of all-time easy-to-prepare favourites, and your baby, in time, is sure to let you know which are the winners.

Dried-fruit compote

MAKES: *12 portions*
PREPARATION TIME: *5 minutes*
COOKING TIME: *30 minutes*
FREEZING: *recommended*

INGREDIENTS
60 g (2 oz) each dried apricots, apples, peaches and prunes
1 dried fig
1 cm (½ inch) vanilla pod

Dried fruit has concentrated amounts of vitamins and minerals, which are unlocked during cooking. To retain as much of the goodness as possible, purèe the fruit with the cooking liquid.

1 Check the fruit for pips and stems and remove them. Chop the fruit roughly and put it into a saucepan, with the vanilla pod. Pour over enough boiling water to cover the fruit by about 2.5 cm (1 inch).

2 Bring the water to the boil, cover the pan and simmer gently for 25–30 minutes, until tender. Remove the vanilla pod and then purée the fruit until smooth. Allow to cool a little before serving.

Dutch apples

MAKES: *2 portions*
PREPARATION TIME: *5 minutes*
COOKING TIME: *10 minutes*
FREEZING: *not recommended*

Simple apple purée can be perked up with a few sultanas. Their natural sweetness will offset the tart apple, as well as adding some potassium.

INGREDIENTS

10 ml (2 teaspoons) sultanas, rinsed
1 eating apple, peeled, cored and chopped
a tiny pinch of ground cinnamon

1 Soak the sultanas in a little boiling water until plump. Drain them and put them in a saucepan, with the apple, cinnamon and 15 ml (1 tablespoon) of water.

2 Simmer, stirring frequently, for 10 minutes or until the apple is soft. Purée until smooth. Adjust the consistency with freshly boiled water, and allow to cool a little before serving.

Passion pudding

MAKES: *1 portion*
PREPARATION TIME: *5 minutes*
FREEZING: *not recommended*

Passion-fruit may seem a little exotic for a tiny baby, but the fragrant flesh of this fruit purées easily and a little goes a long way.

INGREDIENTS

½ ripe passion-fruit
½ banana

Using a teaspoon, scrape the flesh from the passion-fruit and sieve it to remove the pips. Mash the banana until smooth and then stir in the passion-fruit.

Apricot condé

MAKES: *2 portions*
PREPARATION TIME: *10 minutes*
COOKING TIME: *10 minutes*
FREEZING: *recommended*

Use dried, canned or fresh apricots for this easy dessert.

INGREDIENTS

2 ready-to-eat dried apricots, soaked in 150 ml (¼ pint) freshly boiled water, or 1 canned or fresh apricot, peeled and stoned
30 ml (2 tablespoons) flaked rice
150 ml (¼ pint) baby milk

Purée the apricot, with the soaking water (if used), until smooth. Cook the rice as for Rice Pudding (see page 33). Stir in the apricot purée and mix well. Allow to cool a little before serving.

CHAPTER 2

Infants

8 - 18 MONTHS

This is a period of rapid development for your baby. He or she will have started to sit in a high chair and will no longer need to be held during feeding. Even the younger baby will have started to cut a few teeth, while older ones can probably chew fairly chunky foods.

Choosing utensils

Now is the time to encourage children to feed themselves and to try drinking from a cup. If you haven't yet bought any special feeding dishes, consider buying a couple of unbreakable bowls and lidded cups with spouts. Choose a cup with a close-fitting lid and a weighted base.

At this stage, most things find their way into a baby's mouth, and your previous rigid sterilizing régime becomes pointless. However, while you can ease off sterilizing bowls and spoons, you should sterilize milk-feeding bottles and teats for up to 18 months. Bacteria can breed in the warm environment of the bottle and you must always pay special attention to cleaning the bottle and inside the teat.

Unbreakable plastic-lidded cups, with or without handles, are the ideal containers for toddlers' drinks.

Fads and fancies

The baby won't eat lumps

For babies around eight months old, you will still need to purée food to a soft, fairly smooth consistency that toothless gums can chew. As more teeth gradually appear, you can start to make the mixture coarser. Feeding problems often begin when you make this transition. Your baby is used to soft feeds, and, though they may want to bite more, a sturdy toy or teething ring is often preferred.

Encourage chewing by providing sticks of raw vegetables, such as carrot, cucumber or celery, and start to mash food with a fork, rather than blending it in the food processor. If your baby flatly refuses to eat a coarser mixture, begin by adding some mashed or grated food to the usual purée and gradually work up to a rougher texture.

The baby will only eat one thing

It is surprising how a young baby can quickly adopt a fancy for one food above all others. Opinions on this problem vary: many professionals take the line that if the baby is still drinking milk and appears happy and healthy, there is no reason to make a fuss; if you ignore it they will grow out of it. Others feel that it is important to lead by example: the sight of the family enjoying mealtimes together, and eating a variety of interesting foods, will make the baby want to join in.

The baby won't eat

The leading-by-example strategy is a good one to try first. Babies are good imitators, so prepare your baby's meal as usual and eat your own meal. Make no fuss or comment if the baby refuses the food, simply take it away and try again next time.

Novelty cutters can transform ordinary foods into something more attractive for fussy eaters.

Children are very influenced by colour and always seem to go for brightly coloured foods first. Try to combine some contrasting colours and shapes on their plates. You may like to buy some small petit-four cutters or novelty biscuit cutters in different shapes. Carrot slices and even toast looks more appealing in the shape of a flower or star.

For some reason, the food from Mum or Dad's plate seems tastier and more attractive than the baby's own. Try feeding your baby straight from your own plate for a couple of mealtimes.

For older children who won't eat, forget set mealtimes. Try packing a picnic and eat it together. You don't have to go outdoors. Try throwing an old sheet over the table and sit underneath it in a makeshift tent. Have a teddy bears' picnic or a toy party.

Let them help you prepare the meal or do a spot of baking. Children love to roll out biscuit dough and cut out fancy shapes.

Invite another child of a similar age to lunch or tea; if possible, find one with a good appetite. Try not to give too much praise to the hearty eater, though, or your child may feel overshadowed rather than impressed by their companion.

Finally, remember that refusing food is really only a passing phase: unlike adults, who are conditioned into eating three meals a day, a toddler will only eat when hungry, and, as far as we know, no child has ever starved itself to death through its own stubbornness!

As the menu planner (right) shows by now your baby will be eating more and not relying on milk so much for nourishment. However, as milk contains a concentrated supply of protein and calcium it is important that you give your baby at least 600 ml (pint) daily. This can be in a variety of forms, such as from yogurt and cheese, in cooked dishes and in a bottle for a between-meals drink. As your baby grows, you will need to increase the quantities of food you give at mealtimes.

Menu planner

Your four-week infant mealtime guide

	Breakfast	Late morning	Lunch	Afternoon	Tea	Bedtime
Week 1						
Day 1	Oat Porridge	milk	Cheesy-topped Tomatoes; Baked Banana	fruit yogurt; juice drink	Potato Patacakes	milk
Day 2	fruit yogurt	milk	Three-bean Hash; Honey Squares	Fruit Purée; milk	Mini Macaroni Cheese	milk
Day 3	Vanilla and Raisin Flakes	milk; Apple Jumbles	Pumpkin Puff; milk	Melon Cooler	Cowboy	milk
Day 4	Tot's Toasts	milk	Corn Chowder; Fruity Wibble Wobble	Avocado Cream; juice drink	Buttons and Bows	milk
Day 5	Apple Bix	milk	Sunshine Saucy Pasta; Honey Pudding	fruit purée; milk	Chickadee Puffs	milk
Day 6	Baby Muesli	milk	ABC Cheese; Strawberry Rice	fruit yogurt; juice drink	Couscous Salad	milk
Day 7	Cheese Brunch	milk	Dilly Dhally Semolina Pudding	fruit purée; milk	Creamed Mushrooms	milk
Week 2						
Day 1	Teddy Bear Porridge	milk	Squish Squash; Milky Wibble Wobble	fruit yogurt; juice drink	Cheese Charlotte	milk
Day 2	Apricot Granola	milk	Mix-Up Mushrooms; Baked Bananas	Applejack Afternooner; milk	Creamy Herb Pasta	milk
Day 3	Fresh Fruit Yogurt	milk	Sticky Rice; Pink Coconut Ice	fruit yogurt; juice drink	Cottage Bake	milk
Day 4	Strawberry Crackles	milk	Teeny Tortilla; Orange Custard Cream	Melon Cooler; milk	Potato Patacakes	milk
Day 5	Honey-bunch Brunch	milk	Mini Minestrone; Apple Jumbles	Banana and Date Whip; juice drink	Mini Macaroni Cheese	milk
Day 6	Apple Bix; Honey Pudding	milk	Vegetable Cheese Ribbons	fruit purée; milk	Creamed Mushrooms	milk
Day 7	Tot's Toasts	milk	Leek and Potato Sloop; Strawberry Rice	fruit yogurt; juice drink	Buttons and Bows	milk
Week 3						
Same as week 1						
Week 4						
Same as week 2						

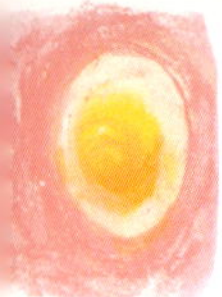

BREAKFASTS

As babies get older and more mobile, they will be hungrier in the mornings. Now is the time to start introducing more substantial breakfasts. Breakfast time can be a somewhat frantic affair, if you are trying to placate a hungry baby while simultaneously attempting to get ready what they are screaming for. These recipes are fast and fuss-free, and many can even be made a day or so before.

Cheese brunch

MAKES: *1 portion*
PREPARATION TIME: *8 minutes*
FREEZING: *not recommended*

INGREDIENTS

- *1 small apple, peeled, cored and grated*
- *30 g (1 oz) mild Cheddar cheese, grated*
- *30 g (1 oz) sultanas*
- *15 ml (1 tablespoon) Greek-style yogurt*
- *2.5 ml (½ teaspoon) bran flakes, crushed*

Try to alternate your baby's breakfast with cereal- and fruit-based dishes occasionally. This is a nice mix of the two and couldn't be easier and quicker to prepare.

Put all the ingredients, except the bran flakes, in a blender or food processor and blend briefly. Spoon into a bowl and sprinkle over the bran flakes before serving.

HINTS AND TIPS

Cheese Brunch can be made and stored in the fridge overnight.

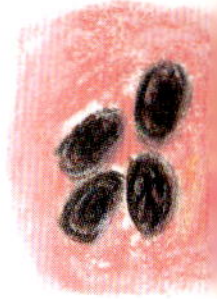

Oat porridge

Real porridge has no match in my view; the natural oats combined with milk have their own sweetness. This makes porridge a popular breakfast for babies and it's a healthy choice, as you don't have to sweeten it. Oats are high in soluble fibre, too, so porridge is an ideal breakfast for you and the rest of the family, too.

1 Put the milk in a small saucepan and bring it to the boil. Sprinkle in the rolled oats and stir well.
2 Continue to stir over a low heat until the porridge is thick and creamy. Leave the porridge to cool for a few minutes before feeding your baby. Adjust the consistency with cold milk, if necessary, if the porridge is too thick.

Makes: *1 portion*
Preparation time: *2 minutes*
Cooking time: *5 minutes*
Freezing: *not recommended*

Ingredients
150 ml (¼ pint) milk
15 ml (1 tablespoon) organic rolled oats

Teddy bear porridge

A little puréed pear provides extra vitamins, while the honey will add flavour and sweetness.

1 Put the pear in a saucepan with 10 ml (2 teaspoons) water. Cook over a medium heat for 5 minutes, or until softened. Mash with a fork. Add the milk and bring to the boil.
2 Sprinkle in the oats and stir over a low heat until thickened and creamy. Stir in the honey then allow to cool for a few minutes before feeding your baby.

Makes: *1 portion*
Preparation time: *5 minutes*
Cooking time: *10 minutes*
Freezing: *not recommended*

Ingredients
1 pear, peeled, cored and chopped
150 ml (¼ pint) milk
20 ml (4 teaspoons) organic rolled oats
1.25 ml (¼ teaspoon) clear honey

Hints and tips
Purée the pear before adding it to the teddy bear porridge if your baby is still unable to eat "bits".

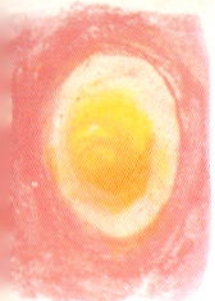

Baby muesli

MAKES: *3 portions*
PREPARATION TIME: *15 minutes + overnight soaking*
FREEZING: *not recommended*

INGREDIENTS
30 g (1 oz) each wheatgerm and rolled oats
115 ml (4 fl oz) unsweetened apple, orange or pineapple juice
5 ml (1 teaspoon) clear honey
60 g (2 oz) sultanas
1 dried peach, finely chopped
5 ml (1 teaspoon) fromage frais

A batch of this will keep for three days, stored in an airtight container in the fridge. Vary the flavour according to whatever fruit is available. Most dried fruit is suitable: try dried apricots with orange or tropical fruit juice, dried pear with apple juice or add more vine fruits and use unsweetened grape juice. Watch out, this breakfast dish has a strange habit of disappearing when there are adults about.

1 Soak the wheatgerm and oats in the fruit juice for a couple of hours. Stir in the honey and dried fruits. Leave to soak overnight.
2 Purée a portion in a blender or food processor for about 30 seconds. Stir in the fromage frais before serving.

Fresh fruit yogurt

MAKES: *1 portion*
PREPARATION TIME: *10 minutes*
FREEZING: *not recommended*

INGREDIENTS
15 ml (1 tablespoon) puréed fruit
60 ml (4 tablespoons) natural yogurt
1.25 ml (¼ teaspoon) vanilla extract
1.25 ml (¼ teaspoon) clear honey
1.25 ml (¼ teaspoon) wheatgerm

Ready-prepared pots of fruit yogurt can often be an expensive and wasteful purchase if your baby doesn't like the flavour you've selected. It's easy to make your own using your baby's favourites and at least these won't be laced with sugar, as ready-made ones often are.

Mix together the fruit, yogurt, vanilla extract and honey. Spoon into a bowl and sprinkle the wheatgerm on top.

HINTS AND TIPS
For older babies, try using unpuréed fruits. Hulled and mashed strawberries or raspberries work well.

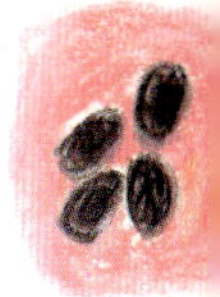

Apricot granola

Similar to muesli, granola is a mix of dried fruits, toasted nuts and cereals. Make a batch and store it in an airtight container. Then, the night before, simply soak what you need in milk, fruit juice or yogurt.

MAKES: *6 adult portions*
PREPARATION TIME: *10 minutes + overnight soaking*
COOKING TIME: *8 minutes*
FREEZING: *not recommended*

INGREDIENTS
85 g (3 oz) wheatgerm
45 g (1½ oz) each rolled oats and bran flakes
15 g (½ oz) ground almonds
60 g (2 oz) ready-to-eat dried apricots, chopped finely
30 g (1 oz) sultanas
a pinch of ground cinnamon
Grated zest of 1 small orange

1 Preheat the oven to Gas Mark 6/200°C/400°F. Spread the wheatgerm, oats, bran flakes and almonds in a single layer on a baking sheet. Bake for 5 minutes. Stir well and then cook for 3 minutes more, or until the almonds are evenly golden.
2 Spoon into a bowl and leave until completely cool. Add the apricots, sultanas, cinnamon and orange rind to the roasted mixture. Store in airtight container until needed.
3 Soak a portion in 150 ml (¼ pint) liquid overnight.
4 Purée in a blender or food processor for 30 seconds before serving.

Strawberry crackles

Unsweetened commercial cereals are fortified with vitamins and minerals and can be a great standby when time is really short. Buy small tester packets if possible, and, if all else fails, the baby can always play with the box.

MAKES: *1 portion*
PREPARATION TIME: *5 minutes + 10 minutes soaking*
FREEZING: *not recommended*

INGREDIENTS
3 small strawberries, washed and hulled
45 ml (3 tablespoons) puffed rice cereal
150 ml (¼ pint) warm milk

Finely chop the strawberries and then mash them until smooth. Mix them with the cereal and warm milk. Leave to soak for 10 minutes before feeding the baby.

HINTS AND TIPS
Use canned or thawed frozen fruit when strawberries are out of season. Purée it in a food processor or blender if necessary.

Apple bix

Makes: *1 portion*
Preparation time: *5 minutes*
Cooking time: *8 minutes*
Freezing: *not recommended*

Ingredients
- *1 small dessert apple, peeled, cored and chopped, or, 1 cube of apple purée, thawed*
- *1 rusk or rice cake or ½ a Weetabix*
- *150 ml (¼ pint) milk*

Use unsweetened rusk, rice cakes or Weetabix as the basis of this simple breakfast and if you've a batch of apple purée in the freezer, all the better. Try to remember to defrost a cube in the fridge overnight.

1 Put the apple in a saucepan with 10 ml (2 teaspoons) water and cook over a low heat for 5–6 minutes, or until softened. Mash well with a fork.

2 Crumble the rusk, rice cake or Weetabix into the apple and then stir in the milk. Stir over low heat until just warmed. Spoon into a serving bowl.

Vanilla and raisin flakes

Makes: *1 portion*
Preparation time: *5 minutes + overnight soaking*
Freezing: *not recommended*

Ingredients
- *15 ml (1 tablespoon) Californian sun-dried raisins*
- *45 ml (3 tablespoons) natural yogurt*
- *15 ml (1 tablespoon) milk*
- *15 ml (1 tablespoon) each bran flakes and cornflakes*
- *1.25 ml (¼ teaspoon) vanilla extract*

The B vitamins play an important role in a young baby's diet; they are essential for growth and a baby is using much of the vitamin B intake to do just that. Dried fruit and whole-grain cereals are a rich source of B vitamins and a good way to include them in your baby's daily menu.

1 Mix all the ingredients together. Cover and chill overnight.

2 Purée in a food processor or blender for 30 seconds, or until smooth.

Hints and tips

This may be a little chilly for some babies to eat first thing in the morning, so spoon it into a warmed serving bowl first.

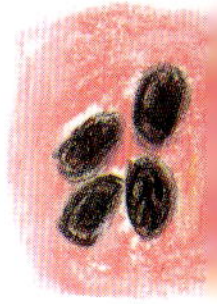

Tot's toasts

MAKES: *1 portion*
PREPARATION TIME: *3 minutes*
FREEZING: *not recommended*

This recipe gives you two options in one. For younger babies, soak the toasts in milk to soften them, and then feed the mixture to your baby with a spoon. When your child is a little older, and has some teeth and is starting to chew, offer fingers of toast to hold and gnaw on. Try using biscuit cutters to cut the toast into fun shapes, such as stars and animals, instead of fingers.

INGREDIENTS
2.5 ml (½ teaspoon) unsalted butter or margarine
1.25 ml (¼ teaspoon) tahini paste
1.25 ml (¼ teaspoon) smooth peanut butter
1 thin slice of wholemeal bread, toasted
a pinch of sesame seeds

1 Preheat the grill to high. Spread the butter, tahini paste and peanut butter over the toasted bread to cover it completely. Sprinkle over the sesame seeds and toast until just golden.
2 Cool slightly before serving.

Honey-bunch brunch

MAKES: *1 portion*
PREPARATION TIME: *5 minutes*
FREEZING: *not recommended*

This is the type of breakfast that slips down easily, so it is great for babies who have yet to cut any teeth.

INGREDIENTS
½ banana, peeled
2 canned prunes, stoned
10 ml (2 teaspoons) Greek-style yogurt
10 ml (2 teaspoons) natural cottage cheese
2.5 ml (½ teaspoon) clear honey
a pinch of grated nutmeg

Put all the ingredients in a food processor and blend them briefly until smooth.

HINTS AND TIPS

A variation of this is to replace the banana with avocado, and the prunes with half a canned peach. Serve both varieties soon after making or they will discolour.

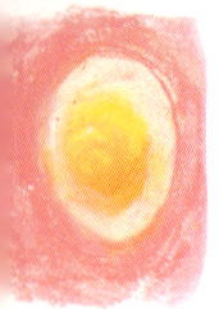

8-18
MONTHS

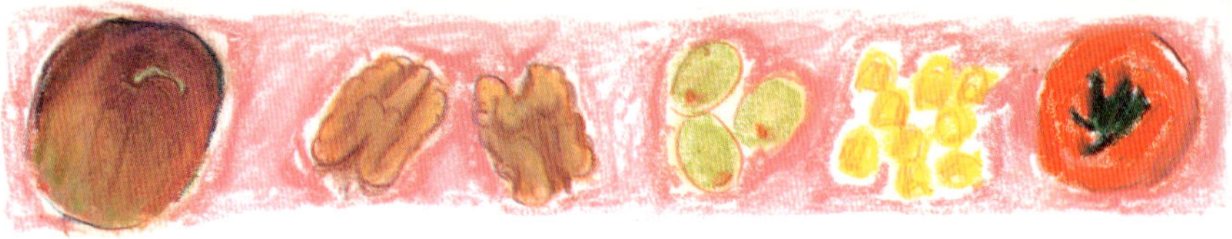

LUNCHES

Now your baby is moving on from mainly milk feeds, it is essential that you maintain the correct balance of body-building and energy-giving foods. Lunch is generally considered to be a baby's main meal of the day and, in this section, protein-rich meals, based on ground nuts, beans and pulses, are featured. Combined with a sensible strategy for other meals, these ideas will ensure your baby stays well nourished.

Three-bean hash

MAKES: *4 portions*
PREPARATION TIME: *15 minutes + overnight soaking*
COOKING TIME: *45 minutes*
FREEZING: *recommended*

INGREDIENTS
30 g (1 oz) each butter beans and chick-peas
60 g (2 oz) French beans, trimmed and chopped
5 ml (1 teaspoon) sunflower oil
60 g (2 oz) carrot, peeled and chopped
60 g (2 oz) swede, peeled and cubed
115 g (4 oz) potato, peeled and cubed
60 ml (4 tablespoons) vegetable stock

Use canned beans for speed, but you must still sieve them before using, to get rid of the indigestible husks.

1 Soak the butter beans and chick-peas in cold water overnight.
2 Drain the pulses and put them in a saucepan. Cover with cold water and bring to the boil. Boil rapidly for 10 minutes.
3 Skim any froth from the surface, reduce the heat and simmer for 35 minutes. Add the French beans, carrots, swede and potato to the pan and cook for a further 10 minutes, or until the beans, chick-peas and vegetables are tender. Drain well.
4 While they are still warm, press the butter beans and chick-peas through a sieve into a bowl. Add the cooked vegetables and mash everything well.
5 Heat the oil in an 18 cm (7-inch) non stick frying pan. Add the vegetable mixture and press down well with the back of a spoon. Cook over a medium heat until the underside is golden. Flip over and cook the second side.
6 Divide the hash into 4 equal pieces. Moisten with a little vegetable stock before serving.

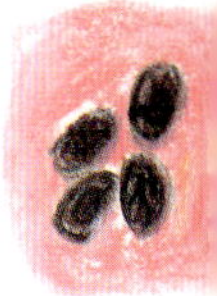

Cheesy-topped tomatoes

The ground almonds help to thicken this baked mixed-vegetable purée, as well as providing essential protein and vitamins.

MAKES: *4 portions*
PREPARATION TIME: *20 minutes*
COOKING TIME: *15 minutes*
FREEZING: *not recommended*

INGREDIENTS
4 firm ripe tomatoes, skinned and de-seeded
1 carrot, peeled and chopped
45 g (1½ oz) Cheddar grated
115 ml (4 fl oz) milk
45 g (1½ oz) ground almonds
a pinch of dried mixed herbs

1 Preheat the oven to Gas Mark 4/180°C/350°F. Chop the tomatoes and steam them with the carrot for 10 minutes, or until tender.
2 Blend the tomatoes and carrot in a food processor or blender, with 30 g (1 oz) of the Cheddar cheese and the milk, ground almonds and herbs; don't make the purée too smooth.
3 Grease four 150 ml (¼-pint) ramekins or ovenproof teacups and spoon in the tomato mixture. Sprinkle the remaining cheese on top and bake for 15 minutes, or until golden. Cool slightly before serving.

Corn chowder

This is a baby-friendly version of the classic New-England recipe. The potato gives it a wonderfully comforting, thick texture, and the corns add sweetness.

MAKES: *6 portions*
PREPARATION TIME: *10 minutes*
COOKING TIME: *15 minutes*
FREEZING: *recommended*

INGREDIENTS
5 ml (1 teaspoon) unsalted butter or margarine
5 cm (2-inch) piece of leek, white part only, sliced
¼ red pepper, de-seeded and finely chopped
300 ml (½ pint) milk
115 g (4 oz) frozen sweetcorn
115 g (4 oz) potato, peeled and chopped
1 bay leaf

1 Melt the butter in a saucepan and cook the leek and pepper over a medium heat for 5 minutes, or until softened. Add the milk, sweetcorn, potato and bay leaf and bring to the boil.
2 Reduce the heat and simmer for 10 minutes or until the potato is tender. Remove the bay leaf and either mash or blend briefly in a food processor or blender.

Vegetable pots

MAKES: *2 portions*
PREPARATION TIME: *10 minutes*
COOKING TIME: *30 minutes*
FREEZING: *not recommended*

INGREDIENTS
30 g (1 oz) cooked mashed broccoli
30 g (1 oz) cooked mashed carrot
30 g (1 oz) cooked unsalted white rice
15 ml (1 tablespoon) grated Cheddar cheese
1 size-3 egg yolk
90 ml (6 tablespoons) milk

These can be made with cooked leftover vegetables or a selection of freshly steamed vegetables.

1 Preheat the oven to Gas Mark 4/180°C/350°F. Grease two 150 ml (¼-pint) ramekins or ovenproof teacups. Mix the vegetables and rice together with 10 ml (2 teaspoons) of the cheese. Stir in the egg and milk and mix everything together.
2 Spoon the mixture into dishes and cover them with foil. Put the dishes in a roasting tin and fill the roasting tin with boiling water to come half-way up the tin. Transfer carefully to the oven and cook for 30 minutes, or until set. Allow to cool slightly before feeding your baby.

Dilly dhally

MAKES: *8 portions*
PREPARATION TIME: *10 minutes*
COOKING TIME: *25 minutes*
FREEZING: *not recommended*

INGREDIENTS
5 ml (1 teaspoon) vegetable oil
½ small onion, peeled and chopped
115 g (4 oz) each carrot, parsnip and potato, peeled and chopped
a pinch each of ground coriander and cumin
60 g (2 oz) red lentils
600 ml (1 pint) vegetable stock

This dish is a great source of protein and inspired by a classic Indian vegetarian recipe. It is also incredibly easy to make.

1 Heat the oil in a saucepan and fry the onion for 5 minutes, or until soft. Add the carrot, parsnip and potato. Sprinkle the spices over and cook for a further 5 minutes.
2 Stir in the lentils and stock and bring to the boil. Cover the pan and leave it to simmer, stirring occasionally, for 25 minutes, or until the lentils are tender.
3 Blend briefly in a food processor or blender until smooth.

HINTS AND TIPS

If the mixture is too thick, adjust it with water or stock. For older babies, serve with unsalted breadsticks for them to hold and dip in the dhal.

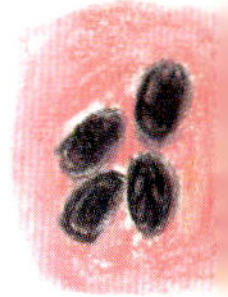

Mushroom surprise

MAKES: *6 portions*
PREPARATION TIME: *15 minutes*
COOKING TIME: *25 minutes*
FREEZING: *not recommended*

Cabbage has quite a strong flavour, which babies can dislike; but when it is combined with a fairly bland partner such as mushrooms, babies should eat it up quite happily.

INGREDIENTS
60 g (2 oz) brown rice
85 g (3 oz) cabbage, shredded
5 ml (1 teaspoon) vegetable oil
4 button mushrooms, wiped and chopped
1 tomato, skinned, de-seeded and chopped
45 g (1½ oz) Cheddar cheese, grated

1 Put the rice in a saucepan and cover with cold water to a depth of about 2.5 cm (1 inch). Bring the water to the boil, reduce the heat, cover the rice and let it simmer for 25 minutes.
2 Add the shredded cabbage to the saucepan and cook for 5 minutes, or until the rice and cabbage are tender.
3 Meanwhile, heat the oil in a frying-pan and cook the mushrooms for 5 minutes. Stir in the tomatoes and cook for 3 minutes more.
4 Drain the rice and cabbage. Blend them in a food processor or blender with half the mushroom mixture. Spoon into the serving dish. Blend the remaining mushroom mixture with the Cheddar and spoon it on top.

Aubergine pasta

MAKES: *4 portions*
PREPARATION TIME: *20 minutes*
COOKING TIME: *33 minutes*
FREEZING: *not recommended*

Babies and children soon seem to form a great fondness for pasta and you couldn't wish for a more convenient food. More importantly, it has carbohydrate and protein to boost energy and growth.

INGREDIENTS
5 ml (1 teaspoon) sunflower oil
60 g (2 oz) each aubergine and courgette, chopped
1 strip of red pepper, de-seeded and cubed
30 g (1 oz) sweetcorn
30 g (1 oz) button mushrooms, wiped and chopped
225 g (8 oz) canned chopped tomatoes
115 ml (4 fl oz) vegetable stock
60 g (2 oz) pasta shapes, e.g., bows, spirals, quills etc.

1 Heat the oil in a saucepan and cook the aubergine, courgette, pepper, sweetcorn and mushrooms for 8 minutes, or until tender.
2 Stir in the tomatoes and bring to the boil. Reduce the heat, cover and simmer for 15 minutes.
3 Add the stock to the pan and return to the boil. Add the pasta shapes and cook for 10 minutes, or until the pasta is tender.
4 Allow to cool slightly and then blend briefly in a food processor or blender.

Pumpkin puff

MAKES: *4 portions*
PREPARATION TIME: *15 minutes*
COOKING TIME: *25 minutes*
FREEZING: *not recommended*

INGREDIENTS
115 g (4 oz) pumpkin, peeled and de-seeded
60 g (2 oz) each carrot and swede
60 ml (4 tablespoons) orange juice
60 ml (4 tablespoons) milk
1 size-3 egg yolk
30 g (1 oz) toasted pumpkin seeds, finely ground

This bakes to a wonderful rich golden colour, which is very appealing. A good amount of vitamin A comes with this, too.

1 Preheat the oven to Gas Mark 4 180°C/350°F. Grease four 150 ml (¼-pint) ramekins or ovenproof teacups. Chop the pumpkin, carrot and swede into equally sized pieces and steam them for 10 minutes, or until they are tender.
2 Blend the vegetables with the orange juice, milk, egg and ground pumpkin seeds until smooth. Spoon into dishes and bake for 25 minutes, or until set. Cool slightly before serving.

HINTS AND TIPS

Due to the amount of oil they contain, nuts and seeds deteriorate with age. If you don't use them regularly, store them in airtight containers in the freezer and use them from frozen.

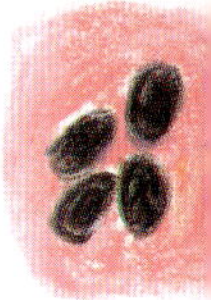

Leek and potato sloop

Soups are a little too liquid to feed to a baby by spoon, but they should be able to manage this slightly thicker version, which contains fresh spinach leaves for iron and colour.

MAKES: *8 portions*
PREPARATION TIME: *15 minutes*
COOKING TIME: *30 minutes*
FREEZING: *not recommended*

INGREDIENTS

15 g (½ oz) unsalted butter
1 young leek, trimmed and chopped
225 g (8 oz) potato, cubed
225 g (8 oz) fresh spinach leaves, shredded
300 ml (½ pint) vegetable stock
15 ml (1 tablespoon) fromage frais

1 Melt the butter in a saucepan and cook the leek over a medium heat for 3–4 minutes, or until softened. Add the potato and the spinach to the pan, with the stock.

2 Bring the mixture to the boil, cover and simmer over a low heat for 30 minutes, stirring occasionally. Mash, or blend briefly in a blender or food processor. Allow the "sloop" to cool slightly, if necessary, and stir in the fromage frais just before serving.

Mix-up mushrooms

Sweet and sour flavours may seem a little sophisticated for a baby's palate, but in fact they love this mild version. This is made with egg-noodles for added protein and carbohydrate.

MAKES: *1 portion*
PREPARATION TIME: *10 minutes*
COOKING TIME: *5 minutes*
FREEZING: *not recommended*

INGREDIENTS

30 g (1 oz) thread egg-noodles
5 ml (1 teaspoon) vegetable oil
4 button mushrooms, wiped and sliced
60 g (2 oz) carrot, peeled and cubed
1 strip each of red and green pepper, de-seeded and chopped
2 canned pineapple chunks, chopped
30 g (1 oz) fresh bean sprouts
60 ml (4 tablespoons) canned chopped tomatoes
5 ml (1 teaspoon) tomato ketchup

1 Put the noodles in a shallow dish and pour over enough boiling water to cover. Leave to soak.

2 Meanwhile, heat the vegetable oil in a frying-pan and stir-fry the mushrooms, carrot and pepper for 4–5 minutes, or until softened.

3 Add the pineapple, bean sprouts and tomatoes and bring to the boil. Stir in the tomato ketchup.

4 Drain the noodles and briefly blend them in a food processor or blender, with the vegetable mixture, until smooth.

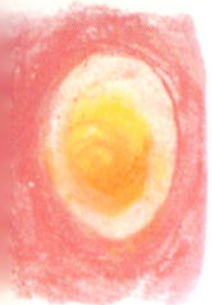

Squish squash

MAKES: *4 portions*
PREPARATION TIME: *10 minutes*
COOKING TIME: *1½ hours*
FREEZING: *not recommended*

INGREDIENTS
1 small butternut squash
60 g (2 oz) each carrot and courgette, cubed
30 g (1 oz) sweetcorn
a pinch of grated nutmeg
a pinch of soft brown sugar
15 g (½ oz) unsalted butter or margarine

Choose small young squash with few blemishes, because older vegetables can be a little bitter. Make these when you have the oven on for baking.

1 Preheat the oven to Gas Mark 4/180°C/350°F. Halve the squash lengthways and scoop out the seeds. Mix the vegetables, nutmeg and sugar together and then use them to fill each squash.
2 Dot the butter over each squash and then wrap them in foil. Put on a baking sheet and cook for 1½ hours, or until the vegetables and squash are tender.
3 Scoop the squash flesh from the skin and mash or blend it briefly in a blender or food processor, with the filling.

Sunshine saucy pasta

MAKES: *6 portions*
PREPARATION TIME: *15 minutes*
COOKING TIME: *20 minutes*
FREEZING: *recommended*

INGREDIENTS
15 g (½ oz) unsalted butter or margarine
½ small onion, peeled and chopped
1 celery stick, washed and finely chopped
¼ each green and red pepper, de-seeded and finely chopped
60 g (2 oz) carrot, peeled and finely chopped
4 firm ripe tomatoes, peeled, de-seeded and chopped
30 g (1 oz) red lentils
150 ml (¼ pint) vegetable stock
a pinch of dried basil
60 g (2 oz) pasta shapes

A simple, full-flavoured tomato sauce that goes well with pasta or baked and then mashed potatoes.

1 Melt the butter in a saucepan and add the onion and celery. Cook over a medium heat for 5 minutes, until softened. Add the pepper, carrot and tomatoes and cook for 5 minutes, stirring occasionally.
2 Stir in the lentils, stock and basil. Bring to the boil, stirring continuously. Reduce the heat, cover the pan and let it simmer for 20 minutes, or until the vegetables and lentils are tender and the sauce thickened.
3 While the sauce is cooking, boil the pasta for 10 minutes, or until tender. Drain well.
4 Blend the sauce and pasta briefly in a food processor or blender.

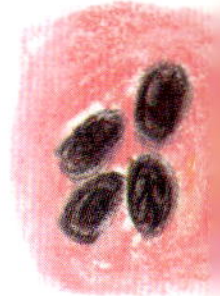

ABC cheese

Crumbled tofu and Gruyère cheese enrich and flavour this simple dish of vegetables in a tasty sauce with a crunchy wheat-flake topping. It is sure to become a favourite.

MAKES: *2 portions*
PREPARATION TIME: *10 minutes*
COOKING TIME: *10 minutes*
FREEZING: *recommended*

INGREDIENTS

60 g (2 oz) aubergine, peeled and cubed
85 g (3 oz) broccoli and cauliflower florets, chopped
1 spring onion, white only, trimmed and chopped
5 ml (1 teaspoon) cornflour
175 ml (6 fl oz) milk
30 g (1 oz) each tofu and Gruyère cheese
15 g (½ oz) wheat flakes, crushed

1 Steam the vegetables for 10 minutes, or until soft.
2 Meanwhile, mix the cornflour with 30 ml (2 tablespoons) of the milk, to form a smooth paste. Heat the remaining milk in a saucepan until boiling.
3 Stir the milk into the cornflour mixture and then return it to the pan. Stir over a low heat until thickened and smooth. Off the heat, crumble in the tofu and grate in half the cheese. Return the pan to the heat and stir until the cheese has melted.
4 Stir the vegetables into the cheese sauce and mash or blend them briefly in a food processor or blender. Spoon into bowls and sprinkle the remaining cheese and wheat flakes on top.

Mini minestrone

I've added a few haricot beans to pep up the protein and provide energy; remember to sieve these first, for babies under nine months.

MAKES: *10 portions*
PREPARATION TIME: *20 minutes*
COOKING TIME: *30 minutes*
FREEZING: *not recommended*

INGREDIENTS

5 ml (1 teaspoon) oil
60 g (2 oz) each carrot, white of leek and celery
115 g (4 oz) potato, cubed
115 g (4 oz) green cabbage, shredded
6 ripe tomatoes, skinned, de-seeded and chopped
600 ml (1 pint) vegetable stock
15 ml (1 tablespoon) peas
15 ml (1 tablespoon) canned or cooked haricot beans
10 ml (2 teaspoons) tomato purée
60 g (2 oz) small pasta stars

1 Heat the oil in a saucepan and fry the carrot, leek and celery for 5 minutes over a medium heat until soft. Add the potato and the cabbage to the pan, with the chopped tomatoes and stock.
2 Cover the pan and bring to the boil. Reduce the heat and simmer for 20 minutes.
3 Stir in the peas, beans, tomato purée and pasta. Return to the boil, and then simmer for 10 minutes, or until the pasta and vegetables are soft.
4 Mash the vegetables or blend briefly in a food processor or blender.

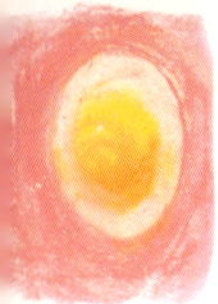

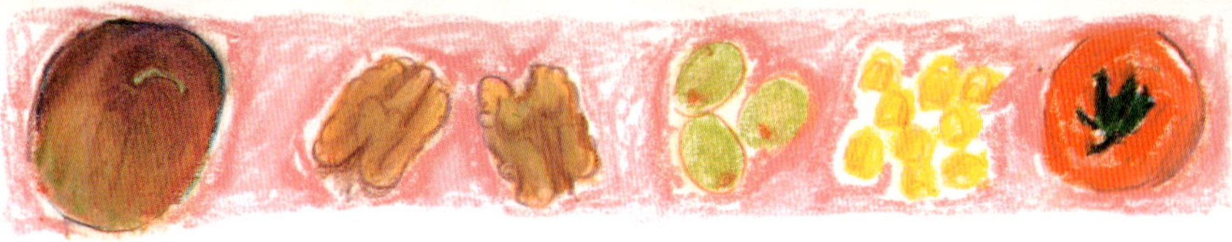

Vegetable cheese ribbons

SERVES: *2*
PREPARATION TIME: *10 minutes*
COOKING TIME: *30 minutes*
FREEZING: *not recommended*

INGREDIENTS
30 g (1 oz) brown rice
150 ml (¼ pint) vegetable stock
60 g (2 oz) each carrot, courgette and green cabbage, shredded
1 tomato, skinned, de-seeded and cut in strips
45 g (1½ oz) Emmenthal cheese, grated

This can be made from a variety of vegetables – whatever you may have to hand. But when making your own combinations, pick starchy and leaf vegetables for the best nutritional balance.

1 Cook the brown rice in the vegetable stock for 20 minutes. Add the carrot and cook for 5 minutes more. Then stir in the courgette and cabbage.
2 Return to the boil and simmer for 5 minutes, or until the rice and vegetables are tender.
3 Stir in the tomato and half the cheese. Blend the rice mixture briefly in a blender or food processor. Spoon it into a serving dish and sprinkle it with cheese.

Sticky rice

MAKES: *4 portions*
PREPARATION TIME: *10 minutes*
COOKING TIME: *38 minutes*
FREEZING: *not recommended*

INGREDIENTS
30 g (1 oz) unsalted butter or margarine
½ small onion, peeled and chopped
60 g (2 oz) rice
60 g (2 oz) broccoli florets
1 strip each of red and yellow pepper, de-seeded and chopped
450 ml (¾ pint) vegetable stock
scant 1.25 ml (¼ teaspoon) Marmite
30 g (1 oz) cashew nuts, ground
15 g (½ oz) fresh Parmesan cheese, grated

Round-grain pudding rice or Italian Arborio rice are the best types to use for this. They cook down to a lovely, creamy consistency, which your baby can digest easily.

1 Melt the butter in a saucepan and cook the onion over a medium heat for 5 minutes or until softened. Stir in the rice, broccoli and peppers. Cook, stirring, for 2–3 minutes.
2 Mix together the stock and Marmite and stir into the rice mixture. Simmer gently for 30 minutes, stirring frequently, until the mixture is thick and nearly all the liquid has been absorbed.
3 Blend briefly in blender or food processor, with the ground cashew nuts and the cheese.

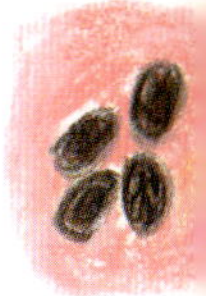

Teeny tortilla

Not the rough Mexican floury type of tortilla, but a soft pancake speckled with parsley.

Makes: *6 pancakes*
Preparation time: *5 minutes*
Cooking time: *15 minutes*
Freezing: *not recommended*

Ingredients
60 g (2 oz) plain flour
1 size-3 egg yolk
300 ml (½ pint) milk
30 ml (2 tablespoons) chopped fresh parsley
10 ml (2 teaspoons) vegetable oil
For the filling:
½ small avocado
1 tomato, skinned, de-seeded and chopped
85 g (3 oz) creamed tomatoes (passata)
10 ml (2 teaspoons) fromage frais

1 Put the flour in a bowl and beat in the egg yolk and milk to form a smooth batter. Stir in the parsley.
2 Heat 5 ml (1 teaspoon) of the oil in an 18-cm (7-inch) non-stick frying-pan. Drain off excess oil and pour in about 1 tablespoon of batter. Swirl the pan so that the mixture evenly coats the base.
3 Cook over a medium heat for 2 minutes, or until the base has set. Flip over and cook the other side. Repeat to make six pancakes in total.
4 Mash the avocado with the chopped tomato. Spread it over one pancake and roll up. Heat the creamed tomatoes and blend them briefly with the stuffed pancake. Mix in fromage frais before feeding to your baby.

Hints and tips

The pancakes will freeze. Interleave them with greaseproof paper and seal them in a polythene bag. Freeze for up to 3 months.

PUDDINGS

A simple selection of quick puddings to help finish mealtimes with a smile. Babies who are teething may lose interest in food, so forget about puddings and offer frozen fruit segments such as apple, pear, orange or melon instead. These are great gum-soothers, which they can suck and chew and be nourished at the same time.

MAKES: *4 portions*
PREPARATION TIME: *10 minutes + chilling overnight*
FREEZING: *not recommended*

INGREDIENTS
2.5 ml (½ teaspoon) Gelozone (vegetable gelling powder)
300 ml (½ pint) fruit juice or purée

HINTS AND TIPS

Colour jelly with natural food colouring pastes for more vibrant effects. To create shapes, pour jelly into a shallow dish and chill until set. Stamp out shapes with biscuit cutters. Letters, numbers and animal shapes are particularly appealing.

Fruity wibble wobble

You can use any fresh fruit juice or purée for this, except pineapple, papaya or kiwi fruit. This is because these fresh fruits have an enzyme that prevents setting. Puréed canned fruits work fine.

1 Pour 60 ml (4 tablespoons) fruit juice into a small bowl and sprinkle in the Gelozone. Mix well until dissolved. Stand the bowl in a saucepan of hot water and leave it until just below boiling point (the liquid should be steaming but not bubbling).
2 Stir the Gelozone into the fruit juice or purée and pour into moulds. Chill overnight until set.

Milky wibble wobble

Soft-fruit purées, such as raspberry or strawberry, seem to work best in this milky jelly.

MAKES: *4 portions*
PREPARATION TIME: *15 minutes + overnight chilling*
FREEZING: *not recommended*

INGREDIENTS
60 g (2 oz) strawberries or raspberries
5 ml (1 teaspoon) icing sugar
150 ml (1/4 pint) water
2.5 ml (1/2 teaspoon) Gelozone (vegetable gelling powder)
150 ml (1/4 pint) milk

1 Hull and chop the fruit. Put into a saucepan with the sugar and water and bring to the boil. Simmer for 10 minutes or until the fruit is very soft.
2 Measure 60 ml (4 tablespoons) of the cooking liquid into a small bowl. Sprinkle in the Gelozone and stir until dissolved. Sieve fruit to remove pips.
3 Blend the fruit, cooking liquid, Gelozone and milk together until frothy. Pour into a serving dish and chill until set.

Strawberry rice

If you can, use short-grain brown rice; it will be more nutritious, with its B vitamins still intact.

MAKES: *4 portions*
PREPARATION TIME: *5 minutes*
COOKING TIME: *30 minutes*
FREEZING: *not recommended*

INGREDIENTS
30 g (1 oz) short-grain brown rice
1.25 ml (1/4 teaspoon) vanilla extract
300 ml (1/2 pint) milk
10 ml (2 teaspoons) low-sugar strawberry spread or fruit purée

1 Put the rice, vanilla extract and milk in a saucepan and bring to just below the boil. Cover and simmer, stirring occasionally, for 30 minutes or until the milk has been absorbed and the rice is tender.
2 Stir in the strawberry purée just before serving.

HINTS AND TIPS

Ready-prepared fruit spreads are similar to jam or jellies but made with little or no sugar; they make a useful standby pudding. Try them with yogurt or fromage frais.

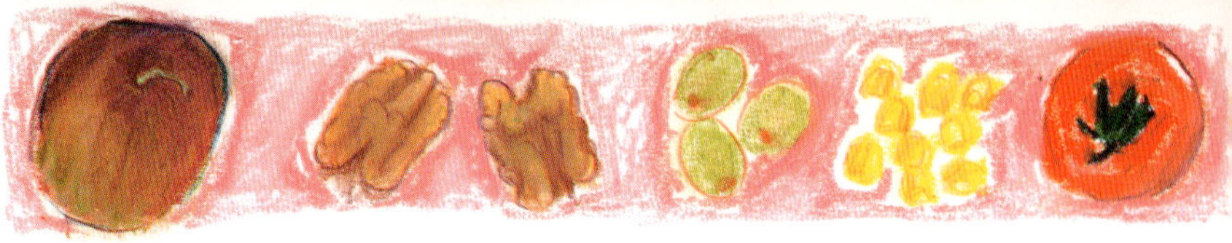

Apple jumbles

MAKES: *2 portions*
PREPARATION TIME: *10 minutes*
COOKING TIME: *20 minutes*
FREEZING: *not recommended*

INGREDIENTS
2 dessert apples, peeled, cored and chopped
15 ml (1 tablespoon) apple juice
30 g (1 oz) sultanas
a pinch of ground cinnamon
30 g (1 oz) each plain flour and rolled oats
10 ml (2 teaspoons) softened unsalted butter or margarine
natural yogurt to serve, if necessary

The oat topping adds a new texture to soft, cooked apples for baby to try. Mix the topping in and let it soften before feeding this to younger babies.

1 Put the apples, apple juice, sultanas and cinnamon in a small saucepan and cook over a medium heat for 10 minutes, or until softened.
2 Meanwhile, mix together the flour, oats and butter to form a crumble. Spoon the apple mixture into two 150 ml (¼-pint) ramekins and put the oat mixture on top. Preheat the grill to high and toast the topping for 3–4 minutes, or until just golden.
3 Stir the oat topping into the apple mixture to combine. Allow to cool before serving. Moisten with a little yogurt if your baby finds the mixture too dry.

Honey squares

MAKES: *16 squares*
PREPARATION TIME: *10 minutes*
COOKING TIME: *30 minutes*
FREEZING: *recommended*

INGREDIENTS
60 g (2 oz) soft margarine
60 g (2 oz) caster sugar
60 g (2 oz) self-raising wholemeal flour
1 egg yolk
15 ml (1 tablespoon) milk
15 ml (1 tablespoon) clear honey
grated rind and juice of 1 small lemon
natural yogurt, to serve

This delicious pudding makes use of an easy all-in-one cake mixture; the lemon and honey syrup makes it deliciously moist.

1 Preheat the oven to Gas Mark 4/180°C/350°F. Grease and line the base of an 18 cm (7-inch), square, shallow tin. Put the margarine, sugar, flour, egg and milk in a bowl and beat until smooth.
2 Spoon the mixture into the tin and level the surface with the back of a spoon. Cook for 30 minutes or until well risen and set.
3 Meanwhile, warm the honey and lemon together. Whilst it is still warm, prick the cake all over with a cocktail stick. Spoon over the honey mixture and leave until just warm. Cut in small squares or fingers. Crumble into a serving bowl and serve with yogurt.

Semolina pudding

Fresh apricots or peaches make a nice contrast to the slightly gritty texture of semolina. Chop them finely and stir them in prior to baking, or make a purée and stir it in just before serving.

1 Preheat the oven to Gas Mark 6/200°C/400°F. Grease a 600 ml (1-pint) ovenproof dish. Finely chop the fruit and put it in a saucepan, with the milk and butter. Heat gently until the butter has melted.
2 Sprinkle in the semolina, stirring continuously. Bring to the boil. Simmer for 3 minutes and then pour into the ovenproof dish. Cook for 30 minutes, or until the batter has set. Allow to cool slightly before serving.

MAKES: *4 portions*
PREPARATION TIME: *10 minutes*
COOKING TIME: *30 minutes*
FREEZING: *not recommended*

INGREDIENTS
2 fresh apricots or 1 peach, peeled and stoned
300 ml (½ pint) milk
15 g (½ oz) unsalted butter or margarine
30 ml (2 tablespoons) semolina
5 ml (1 teaspoon) sugar

Pink coconut ice

A simple iced dessert that doesn't take an age to prepare and can be enjoyed by everyone in the family.

1 Purée the raspberries in a blender or food processor until smooth. Sieve to remove pips. Whip the cream until soft peaks form. Stir in the coconut milk and fruit purée.
2 Pour the mixture into a rigid plastic box, cover and freeze for 2 hours. Using an electric whisk, whip the ice until smooth. Cover and freeze overnight, until solid.

MAKES: *900 ml (1½ pints)*
PREPARATION TIME: *15 minutes + freezing overnight*

INGREDIENTS
450 g (1 lb) raspberries
300 ml (½ pint) whipping cream
400 g can of coconut milk

HINTS AND TIPS
After the final beating, freeze portions in cleaned individual fromage frais pots. Cover well. Remove the ice cream from the freezer 15 minutes before serving, to allow it to soften slightly.

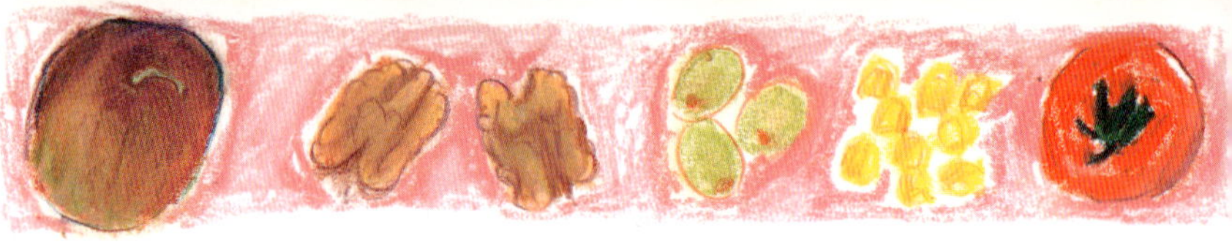

Orange custard cream

MAKES: *2 portions*
PREPARATION TIME: *20 minutes*
COOKING TIME: *1 hour*
FREEZING: *recommended*

INGREDIENTS
300 ml (½ pint) milk
2.5 ml (½ teaspoon) vanilla extract
2 egg yolks
45 g (1½ oz) sugar
grated rind of 1 orange

This can be served warm or chilled according to your baby's preferences. A batch will keep for up to 1 month in the freezer.

1 Preheat the oven to Gas Mark 6/200°C/400°F. Heat the milk until it is almost boiling. Meanwhile, mix together the vanilla, egg yolks, sugar and orange rind. Whisk the milk into the orange mixture.
2 Pour into two 150 ml (¼-pint) ramekins or ovenproof teacups. Put in a small roasting tin and fill the roasting tin with boiling water to come half-way up the sides of the dishes.
3 Cook for 1 hour, or until just set. Serve with puréed or frozen orange segments.

Baked banana

MAKES: *1 portion*
PREPARATION TIME: *5 minutes*
COOKING TIME: *10 minutes*
FREEZING: *not recommended*

INGREDIENTS
1 small banana, sliced
5 ml (1 teaspoon) unsalted butter
2.5 ml (½ teaspoon) lemon juice
1.25 ml (¼ teaspoon) soft brown sugar
a pinch of ground cinnamon
fromage frais, to serve

If your baby enjoys bananas, one day, you'll find a teenager in your kitchen making this recipe.

1 Preheat the oven to Gas Mark 4/180°C/350°F. Grease a 15 cm (6-inch) square of foil and place the banana in the centre. Dot with butter then sprinkle the lemon juice, brown sugar and cinnamon over.
2 Wrap over and seal the foil parcel. Put in a baking dish and cook for 10 minutes, or until softened. Spoon into a serving dish and mash if necessary. Serve with a little fromage frais.

TEA

Your inspiration and energy can be flagging towards the end of the day, so here is a variety of savouries and a few sweet ideas for your baby to try. Many can be made in advance.

Cheese charlotte

A charlotte is a sweet or savoury dish, baked in a mould. The cheesy custard in this version will make this a favourite.

MAKES: *4*
PREPARATION TIME: *25 minutes*
COOKING TIME: *30 minutes*
FREEZING: *recommended*

INGREDIENTS
6 thin slices of wholemeal bread
85 g (3 oz) cream cheese
1 egg yolk
300 ml (½ pint) milk
15 g (½ oz) Cheddar cheese, grated

1 Preheat the oven to Gas Mark 4/180°C/350°F. Grease four 150 ml (¼ pint) ramekins or heatproof dishes. Using a 7.5-cm (2½-inch) biscuit cutter, stamp out 12 rounds from the bread. Spread cream cheese over each round.
2 Put three cheesy rounds, cheese-side up, in each ramekin. Beat the egg and milk together and then pour some over each ramekin. Sprinkle Cheddar on top.
3 Place the ramekins in a roasting tin and fill the tin with enough boiling water to come half way up the side of each dish. Cover with foil and bake for 30 minutes or until set. Cool slightly before serving.

Banana and date whip

This is suitable for tea, or for pudding after a light lunch. Try it with other fruit spreads.

MAKES: *1 portion*
PREPARATION TIME: *5 minutes*
FREEZING: *not recommended*

INGREDIENTS
1 small banana
5 ml (1 teaspoon) date spread
30 ml (2 tablespoons) vanilla custard or yogurt

Mash half the banana with the date spread until smooth. Stir in the custard. Chop the remaining banana finely and then stir it into the mashed-banana mixture.

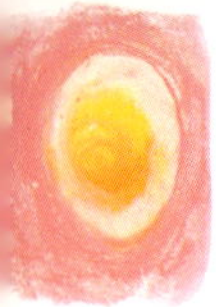

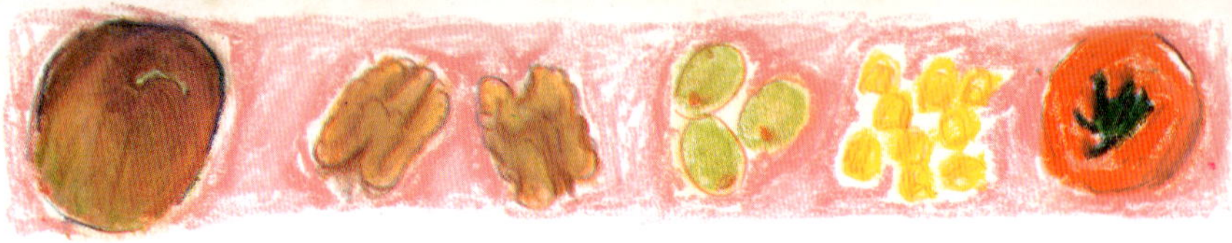

Creamy herb pasta

Makes: *4 portions*
Preparation time: *20 minutes*
Freezing: *not recommended*

Ingredients
300 ml (½ pint) milk
1 teaspoon (5 ml) cornflour
30 ml (2 tablespoons) chopped fresh parsley
a pinch of ground nutmeg
60 g (2 oz) cream cheese
60 g (2 oz) small animal-shaped pasta

This makes quite a thin sauce to coat the pasta, but it will thicken as it cools.

1 Mix 30 ml (2 tablespoons) of milk with the cornflour to form a smooth paste. Heat the remaining milk almost to boiling point and then stir in the cornflour.
2 Return to the saucepan and stir over a low heat or until the mixture bubbles and thickens. Stir in the parsley, nutmeg and cream cheese.
3 Meanwhile, cook the pasta in boiling water for 8 minutes or as directed on the packet. Drain and stir into the sauce. Chop or blend briefly in a blender or food processor.

Couscous salad

Makes: *4 portions*
Preparation time: *10 minutes + 15 minutes soaking*
Cooking time: *5 minutes*
Freezing: *not recommended*

Ingredients
60 g (2 oz) couscous
30 g (1 oz) raisins
150 ml (¼ pint) hot vegetable stock
1 strip each of red and green pepper, de-seeded and chopped
30 g (1 oz) sweetcorn
1 firm ripe tomato, skinned, de-seeded and chopped
For the dressing:
10 ml (2 teaspoons) sunflower oil
5 ml (1 teaspoon) smooth peanut butter
2.5 ml (½ teaspoon) lemon juice

Cracked wheat or bulghar wheat makes a great base for a baby's first salad. If you prefer, use cooked brown rice.

1 Soak the couscous and raisins in the stock for 15 minutes.
2 Drain the stock into a saucepan through a heatproof sieve. Add 150 ml (¼ pint) water to the retained stock and bring to the boil. Add the peppers and sweetcorn.
3 Position the sieve containing the couscous and raisins over the pan, cover, and steam for 5 minutes, or until the vegetables and couscous are tender.
4 Meanwhile, mix the oil, peanut butter and lemon juice in a bowl.
5 Drain the vegetables and couscous and stir them into the dressing. Chop or blend briefly in a blender or food processor.

Chickadee puffs

MAKES: *12 puffs*
PREPARATION TIME: *15 minutes*
COOKING TIME: *30 minutes*
FREEZING: *not recommended*

Ready-prepared hummus, which is made from a purée of chick-peas and sesame seeds, adds protein and flavour to these tempting morsels and the sesame-seed topping brings the flavour out. Try this with other vegetables as well. The fresh tomato is a cooling and refreshing accompaniment, which also increases the level of vitamin C in the dish.

INGREDIENTS
225 g (8 oz) potato, peeled and chopped
15 g (½ oz) unsalted butter or margarine
15 ml (1 tablespoon) milk
15 ml (1 tablespoon) hummus
1.25 ml (¼ teaspoon) sesame seeds
1 tomato, skinned, de-seeded and chopped

1 Cook the potato in boiling, salted water for 15 minutes, or until tender. Drain well and mash with the butter, milk and hummus.
2 Preheat the oven to Gas Mark 6/200°C/400°F. Lightly grease a 12-hole bun tin. Put a spoonful of potato mixture in each section and sprinkle with sesame seeds. Cook for 15 minutes, or until the top is golden. Serve with the chopped tomato.

Buttons and bows

MAKES: *4 portions*
PREPARATION TIME: *10 minutes*
COOKING TIME: *20 minutes*
FREEZING: *recommended*

Tiny button mushrooms and bow-shaped pasta in a simple tomato sauce make a great tea for babies with hearty appetites.

INGREDIENTS
15 g (½ oz) unsalted butter or margarine
4 firm ripe tomatoes, skinned, de-seeded and chopped
30 g (1 oz) celery, washed and finely chopped
30 g (1 oz) carrot, finely chopped
45 g (1½ oz) button mushrooms, wiped and chopped
60 g (2 oz) bow-shaped pasta
30 g (1 oz) mozzarella cheese, cut in tiny pieces

1 Melt the butter in a saucepan and add the tomatoes, celery and carrot. Simmer gently for 10 minutes.
2 Stir in the mushrooms and cook for a further 5 minutes, or until the vegetables are soft.
3 Meanwhile, cook the pasta in boiling water for 10 minutes, or until tender. Drain well. Stir into the mushroom mixture, with the mozzarella. Chop or blend briefly in blender or food processor.

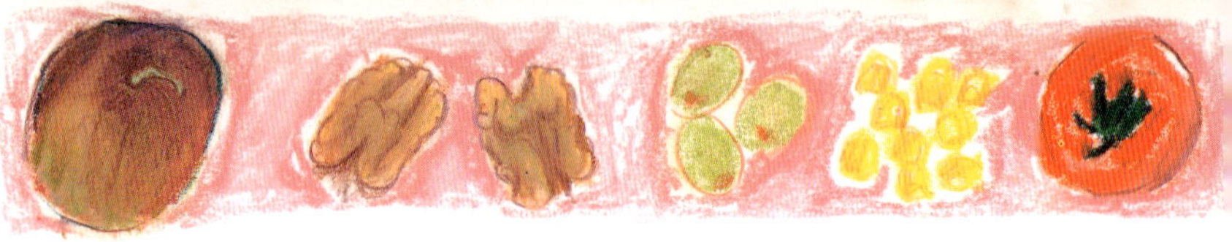

MAKES: *4 portions*
PREPARATION AND COOKING TIME: *35 minutes*
FREEZING: *recommended*

INGREDIENTS
300 ml (1/2 pint) milk
1 bay leaf
115 g (4 oz) macaroni or small pasta shapes
30 g (1 oz) unsalted butter or margarine
30 g (1 oz) flour
60 g (2 oz) Gruyère cheese, grated

Mini macaroni cheese

My son virtually lived on this when he was 7 months old. It is high in calcium, and I account for his good teeth by his early predilection for this recipe.

1 Heat the milk with the bay leaf until almost boiling. Remove from the heat, cover and leave to infuse.
2 Cook the macaroni in boiling water for 10 minutes, or as directed on the packet, until tender. Drain well.
3 Melt the butter in a clean pan, remove from the heat and stir in the flour. Remove the bay leaf from the milk and discard it. Gradually stir the milk into the pan.
4 Stir the sauce over a medium heat until thickened. Simmer for 3 minutes and then stir in half the cheese and all the macaroni. Spoon into four 150 ml (1/4-pint) ramekins or heatproof dishes. Preheat the grill to high.
5 Sprinkle the remaining cheese over each and cook under the grill until golden.

MAKES: *1 portion*
PREPARATION TIME: *5 minutes*
FREEZING: *not recommended*

INGREDIENTS
half a ripe avocado
2.5 ml (1/2 teaspoon) lemon juice
30 g (1 oz) cottage cheese
2.5 ml (1/2 teaspoon) date spread

Avocado cream

Avocados are little orbs of pure energy and packed with vitamins. They mash superbly and will marry with a variety of other flavours quite happily. Lemon juice prevents avocado from discolouring.

1 Using a teaspoon, scoop out the avocado flesh from the skin and mash it with the lemon juice, cottage cheese and date spread.
2 Spoon back into the skin or spoon into the feeding bowl.

HINTS AND TIPS

As a baby will only manage half of an avocado at a sitting, retain the stone in the uneaten piece, sprinkle with lemon juice and wrap in non-PVC film. Keep chilled and eat within 24 hours.

Creamed mushrooms

The egg-yellow oyster or chanterelle mushrooms cook to a lovely, creamy texture and make a tasty change from the cultivated varieties in this version of a traditional teatime favourite. If you can't get them, though, any kind of mushroom can be used; the flavour is better if you can use more than one variety.

1 Cook the mushrooms and onion in melted butter for 5 minutes, or until softened. Mix together the cornflour and milk and stir them into the pan.
2 Stir over a low heat until the sauce thickens. Crumble in the rice cake and stir well. Leave for a few minutes before serving to allow the rice cake to soften somewhat.

MAKES: *1 portion*
PREPARATION TIME: *5 minutes*
COOKING TIME: *5 minutes*
FREEZING: *not recommended*

INGREDIENTS
30 g (1 oz) mushrooms, chopped
1 spring onion, white part only, finely chopped
15 g (½ oz) unsalted butter or margarine
5 ml (1 teaspoon) cornflour
115 ml (4 fl oz) milk
½ unsalted rice cake

Applejack afternooner

Good old apple purée comes into its own again, because it is so versatile and nutritious.

1 Cook the flaked rice in simmering milk for 10 minutes, stirring occasionally, until thickened. Stir in the apple purée, ground almonds and almond essence.
2 Cool a little before serving.

MAKES: *1 portion*
PREPARATION TIME: *3 minutes*
COOKING TIME: *10 minutes*
FREEZING: *not recommended*

INGREDIENTS
15 ml (1 tablespoon) flaked rice
150 ml (¼ pint) milk
60 g (2 oz) apple purée
5 ml (1 teaspoon) ground almonds
½ drop almond essence

HINTS AND TIPS
For older babies, substitute raw grated apple for the apple purée.

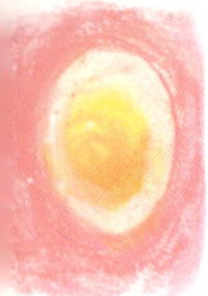

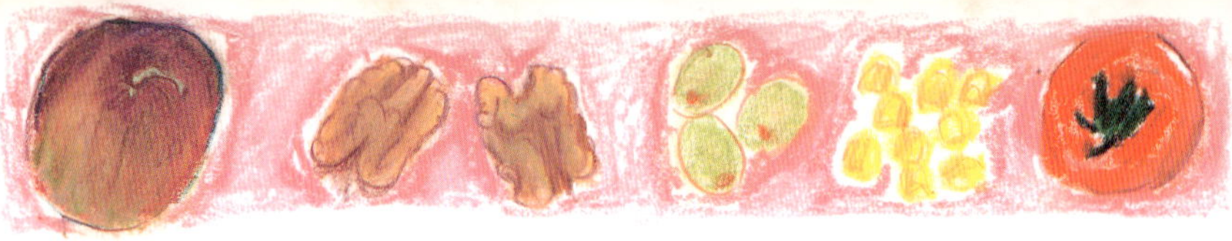

Cottage bake

MAKES: *1 portion*
PREPARATION TIME: *10 minutes*
COOKING TIME: *1 hour*
FREEZING: *not recommended*

INGREDIENTS
175 g (6 oz) potato, scrubbed
15 ml (1 tablespoon) cottage cheese
30 g (1 oz) carrot, grated
30 g (1 oz) courgette, grated

It's not worth putting your oven on to cook just one potato, but this is a good dish to make when the oven is on for baking.

1 Preheat the oven to Gas Mark 6/200°C/400°F. Prick the potato and bake it in the oven for 1 hour, or until tender. Halve and scoop out the flesh with a teaspoon.
2 Mash together the potato, cottage cheese, carrot and courgette. Spoon back into potato skin or feeding bowl.

Cowboy beans

MAKES: *1 portion*
PREPARATION TIME: *5 minutes*
COOKING TIME: *3 minutes*
FREEZING: *not recommended*

INGREDIENTS
45 ml (2 tablespoons) baked beans in tomato sauce
15 ml (1 tablespoon) cooked or canned red kidney beans
2.5 ml (½ teaspoon) Worcestershire sauce
1 thin slice of wholemeal bread
5 ml (1 teaspoon) softened unsalted butter or margarine
yeast extract, for spreading

Some babies may find this a little indigestible, so feed it to babies over 9 months.

1 Heat all the beans and Worcestershire sauce. Mash or blend them briefly in a blender or food processor.
2 Meanwhile, toast the bread. Using a star-shaped biscuit cutter, stamp out shapes and spread with butter and a very thin coating of yeast extract.

HINTS AND TIPS

Try spreading toast with a thin layer of smooth peanut butter as an alternative to yeast extract.

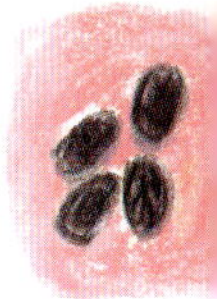

Melon cooler

A refreshing dish for a hot day or to soothe teething gums. Choose a fairly firm-textured melon for this, such as a Charentais or Ogen, as opposed to the more watery types, or the melon ice will not have such a good texture.

MAKES: *1 portion*
PREPARATION TIME: *8 minutes + freezing overnight*
FREEZING: *not recommended*

INGREDIENTS
1/8th of a melon, skinned and de-seeded
150 ml (1/4 pint) milk
15 g (1/2 oz) flaked coconut
extra melon, chopped, or fruit purée, to serve

1 Line an 18-cm (7-inch) square, shallow dish with non-PVC film. Blend the melon, milk and coconut in a blender or food processor until smooth. Pour into the dish, cover and freeze overnight.
2 Put the melon ice in a bowl and crush it with the base of a rolling pin. Serve with extra chopped melon or fruit purée.

Potato patacakes

Make these in the morning, or when you have some mashed potato left over. Once made, they cook quickly.

MAKES: *6 patacakes*
PREPARATION TIME: *15 minutes*
COOKING TIME: *30 minutes*
FREEZING: *not recommended*

INGREDIENTS
225 g (8 oz) potato, peeled and chopped
85 g (3 oz) frozen chopped mixed vegetables, e.g., peas, sweetcorn, peppers, green beans, celery
15 g (1/2 oz) unsalted butter or margarine
15 ml (1 tablespoon) milk
45 g (1 1/2 oz) wholemeal breadcrumbs
45 g (1 1/2 oz) ground almonds
10 ml (2 teaspoons) oil

1 Cook the potato in boiling water for 15 minutes. Add the mixed vegetables and return to the boil. Simmer for 5 minutes or until the vegetables are tender. Drain well.
2 Mash the vegetables with butter and milk until fairly smooth. Using dampened hands, divide the mixture into six portions and shape into rounds.
3 Mix the breadcrumbs and ground almonds together and use to coat each patacake. Chill until required.
4 Heat the oil in a large, non-stick frying-pan. Fry the patacakes for 4–5 minutes each side, until golden. Drain on kitchen paper. Cool for a few minutes before serving. Serve with a little tomato ketchup or home-made tomato purée.

CHAPTER 3

Toddlers and children

18 MONTHS ONWARDS

By the time your toddler reaches the second birthday, you will probably have established some form of eating routine and meal times can be more relaxed occasions. You no longer have the bother of sterilizing, and your little one will have become quite adept at feeding him or herself.

Making mealtimes fun

At 18 months, you may like to buy your child its own cutlery set. This encourages more independence, and makes mealtimes fun. It may be tricky to teach the correct way to hold the cutlery at first: toddlers tend to be ambidextrous, so don't be too worried if your child uses the fork and spoon in the same way as the shovel from the sandpit. If you are really keen to encourage proper use of cutlery, look out for the children's cutlery that has raised bumps on the handles, to show where fingers and thumbs should be placed.

You will probably begin to encourage your child to have good table manners without setting out to do so. From the time the child is in the high chair, the phrases "please" and "thank you", or at least "ta", will have been reinforced and so it is only natural that you extend these to the dining table. You will have your own opinion about the importance of formal table manners; the leading-by-example method is usually effective in setting the standards you want. It is not too much to expect that children should be able to say please and thank you by the age of three, before they begin nursery or playgroup; by school age they should be able to leave cutlery in the correct position on the plate at the end of a meal and ask to be excused from the table.

Encourage good table manners by allowing your child to feed him or herself with their own dinner set. For toddlers, a plate with a weighted base helps reduce risk of spills.

Invitations to tea

Nursery school, play group and joining other children for tea or at birthday parties will help your child put these lessons into practice. This will also help him or her to exert independence. As a vegetarian, you may be concerned that your child will be tempted to try the sausages on sticks, ham rolls and chicken nuggets that are often available at these gatherings. To overcome this, let the nursery school or play group know of your preferences for your child's food. If no provision is made for a vegetarian meal (and nowadays there often is) it is a good idea to pack a lunch box for your child to take. Brightly coloured sandwich boxes are available from most major stores, and will make the owner feel very grown up. Mysteriously, food always seems to disappear from a sandwich box, so if your child is a fussy eater, you may like to try packing a lunch box even for eating at home. Tea or birthday parties may be a little more awkward, as you do not wish to offend the hosts or make your child appear the odd one out. Honesty is the best policy: simply tell the parents that your child is vegetarian and keep your fingers crossed that they steer the meat dishes away. Anyway, even the youngest of vegetarians, offered a choice, tends to stick to the foods that are familiar.

Pack them off to school with their own plastic easy-clean lunch box! Many children prefer to eat a home-packed lunch and you will be able to control what they are eating away from home.

Menu planner

Your four-week toddler mealtime guide

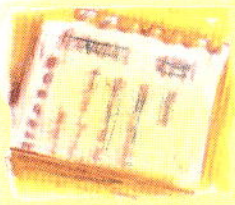

Week 1	Breakfast	Lunch	Tea
Day 1	Bran Tub	Aubergine and Lentil Bolognese; fruit fromage frais	Moonbeams
Day 2	Corn Muffins	Stir-fry with Egg Wheels; Rice and Sultana Pudding	Mexican Beans; banana
Day 3	Swiss-style Muesli	Tomato and Spinach Pie; Toffee Creams	Crumpet Clock; canned mandarin oranges and yogurt
Day 4	Alimoes	Barley Pilaff; Easy Apple Pie	Spotty Dogs; Date Bars
Day 5	Speckled Egg-scrambled	Rice Baskets; Surprise Mice	Noughts and Crosses; fruit yogurt
Day 6	Honeydew Refresher	Sloppy Joes; Toffee Creams and apple wedges	Sandwich Snails
Day 7	Mushroom Kedgeree	Vegetable Crunchies; Teeny Trifles	Rarebit Squares; fruit fromage frais
Week 2			
Day 1	Swiss-style Muesli	Vegetable Lasagne; Surprise Mice	Smiley Clown; Frosted Carrot Cake
Day 2	Toast and Dried-fruit spread	Southern-style Rice and Beans; Bread and Butter Pudding	Scorched Corn Cob; fruit yogurt
Day 3	Shredded Wheat and sliced banana	Peanut Powerballs; Easy Apple Pie	Tomato Piperade; Fun Fingers
Day 4	Waffles with Apple Syrup	Mixed Bean and Spinach Pot; Knights, Castles and Custard	Quick Cannelloni; canned peach and yogurt
Day 5	Bran Tub	Spring Rolls; Fried Rice; Teeny Trifle	Spotty Dogs; Fun Fingers
Day 6	Lemon Griddle Cakes	Creamy Corn Pasta Spirals; Toffee Cream	Noughts and Crosses; fresh pear
Day 7	Mushroom Kedgeree	Lightning Burgers; Home-baked Beans; Surprise Mice	Double Deckers; ice cream
Week 3			
Same as week 1			
Week 4			
Same as week 2			

Remember, these menus are just suggestions to help you provide your child with a nutritionally balanced and varied diet. Always provide toddlers with a drink at mealtimes; this is best given after the meal, otherwise, water or juice will fill them up too quickly. Relax this rule during hot weather, and particularly if there's been some strenuous playing. Drinks before bedtime is rather a contentious issue. It shouldn't matter if you have a toddler still in nappies. If you are trying to get your child to stay dry during the night, a drink about an hour before bed is the best idea.

BREAKFASTS

Small children probably have their last meal at four- or five-o'-clock, and they may then not eat until seven-o'-clock the next morning, a gap of 14 hours or more, so breakfast is vitally important. By the time they reach the toddler stage, many children will already have their favourite foods. But you need to balance the week's breakfast menus, to make sure they are getting all the nutrition and energy they need. Serve high-protein, energy-boosting foods, combining fruit with yogurt, bread or cereals.

Lemon griddle cakes

MAKES: *16 griddle cakes*
PREPARATION TIME: *10 minutes*
COOKING TIME: *25 minutes*
FREEZING: *recommended*

INGREDIENTS
FOR THE STRAWBERRY SAUCE:
340 g (12 oz) fresh strawberries, hulled and chopped
15 ml (1 tablespoon) caster sugar
Juice of ½ an orange
FOR THE GRIDDLE CAKES:
60 g (2 oz) self-raising unbleached white flour
60 g (2 oz) self-raising wholemeal flour
1 size-3 egg
150 ml (¼ pint) milk
Grated zest of 1 unwaxed lemon
5 ml (1 teaspoon) corn oil

To save time, prepare the batter the night before and chill it until needed. The fruit sauce boosts the body with vitamins A and C and the griddle cakes, though low in fat, provide energy and fibre.

1 Cook the strawberries in a small saucepan, with the caster sugar and orange juice, for 5 minutes, or until soft. Leave to cool.
2 Sift the flours together, adding the bran left in the sieve to the bowl at the end. Beat the egg and milk together. Make a well in the centre of the flour and stir in the egg mixture and the lemon zest. Beat well until smooth.
3 Heat a non-stick griddle, or a large frying-pan. Add the corn oil, and then wipe away any excess with kitchen paper. Spoon about 5 tablespoonfuls of the batter on to the griddle, allowing room for spreading. Cook for 2–3 minutes over a medium heat, until the surface begins to bubble. Flip the griddle cake over and cook the second side until it is golden.
4 Keep the griddle cake warm in a clean tea towel while you cook the remainder. Serve with the strawberry sauce.

Corn muffins

MAKES: *6 muffins*
PREPARATION TIME: *10 minutes*
COOKING TIME: *15 minutes*
FREEZING: *recommended*

A fun alternative to toast, these individual muffins take no time at all to bake and taste delicious. To save time for another day, make a double batch and freeze what's left. Serve the muffins spread with butter or margarine, and fruit spread.

INGREDIENTS
85 g (3 oz) plain wholemeal flour
85 g (3 oz) cornmeal
7.5 ml (1½ teaspoons) baking powder
1 size-3 egg, beaten
15 ml (1 tablespoon) clear honey
150 ml (¼ pint) milk

1 Preheat the oven to Gas Mark 6/200°C/400°F. Lightly grease a six-section muffin tin with oil. Sift the flour, cornmeal and baking powder together into a mixing bowl, adding the bran left in the sieve to the bowl at the end.

2 Beat together the egg, honey and milk. Make a well in the centre of the dry ingredients and add the egg mixture. Gently stir until the mixture just comes together; take care not to over-beat it, or you will knock out the air and the muffins will not rise.

3 Divide the mixture between the holes in the prepared tin and bake the muffins for 12–15 minutes, or until they are well risen and golden.

MAKES: *4 waffles*
PREPARATION TIME: *10 minutes*
COOKING TIME: *8 minutes*
FREEZING: *not recommended*

INGREDIENTS
60 ml (4 tablespoons) unsweetened apple juice
30 ml (2 tablespoons) clear honey
15 ml (1 tablespoon) light soft brown sugar
45 g (1½ oz) unbleached self-raising white flour
45 g (1½ oz) self-raising wholemeal flour
5 ml (1 teaspoon) caster sugar
1 size-3 egg, separated
15 ml (1 tablespoon) corn oil
150 ml (¼ pint) milk

Waffles with apple syrup

Children love to see these made and are delighted when the waffle magically appears from the iron. The waffles are full of protein, as well as calcium to aid bone development. One point though: serve the accompanying syrup sparingly, as it is high in sugar.

1 Heat the apple juice, honey and brown sugar in a saucepan until they have dissolved. Bring to the boil and boil for 2–3 minutes, or until syrupy. Leave to cool.
2 Sift the flours together, adding the bran left in the sieve at the end to the bowl. Stir in the sugar. Make a well in the centre and add the egg yolk and oil. Gradually beat in the milk to form a smooth batter.
3 Lightly grease the waffle iron with oil. Heat the waffle iron as directed by the manufacturer. Meanwhile, whisk the egg white until soft peaks form. Fold the egg white into the waffle batter.
4 Pour the batter into the waffle iron, close the iron and cook for 2–3 minutes. Turn over (if not using an electric model) and cook the second side until the waffle is golden and can be removed easily. Keep warm while cooking the rest of the batter. Serve the waffles with a little of the apple syrup.

MAKES: *about 450 g (1 lb)*
PREPARATION TIME: *5 minutes*
COOKING TIME: *20 minutes*
FREEZING: *not recommended*

INGREDIENTS
85 g (3 oz) dried peaches, finely chopped
180 g (6 oz) dried stoned dates, finely chopped
180 g (6 oz) ready-to-eat dried apricots, finely chopped
grated zest of ½ unwaxed lemon and ½ unwaxed orange
a pinch of ground cinnamon
150 ml (¼ pint) apple or orange juice

Dried-fruit spread

Dried fruit is a concentrated source of iron, calcium and potassium. Use this easy-to-make spread in place of high-sugar jam. It will keep for up to two weeks in a covered container, if you store it in the refrigerator.

1 Boil a 450 g (1 lb) preserving jar for 3 minutes. Remove from the pan with tongs and then leave the jar to dry in a warm oven while you prepare the spread.
2 Put all the ingredients in a saucepan and bring them to the boil. Reduce the heat and simmer very gently for 20 minutes, stirring occasionally, until the mixture has thickened and the fruit juice has evaporated. Add extra apple or orange juice if the mixture sticks during cooking.
3 Mash the mixture until smooth and then spoon it into the prepared jar. Seal, label and cool. Store in the fridge.

Speckled egg-scramble

SERVES: *1*
PREPARATION TIME: *5 minutes*
COOKING TIME: *5 minutes*
FREEZING: *not recommended*

My son calls these "eggs with grass" but he enjoys the flavour and bright-green colour that the fresh herbs add to humdrum scrambled eggs. Remember to cook the eggs to a firm set for youngsters, because of the danger of salmonella poisoning, and don't give this to children under three years old. Serve with toast, corn muffins or waffles.

INGREDIENTS

5 ml (1 teaspoon) butter or margarine
1 size-3 egg
60 ml (4 tablespoons) milk
10 ml (2 teaspoons) chopped fresh herbs, e.g. parsley, chives or chervil

Melt the butter in a saucepan. Beat the egg and milk together and then stir them into the butter. Sprinkle in the herbs and stir over a low heat until the mixture thickens.

Mushroom kedgeree

SERVES: *2*
PREPARATION TIME: *15 minutes*
COOKING TIME: *35 minutes*
FREEZING: *not recommended*

This can double as a tea as well as a breakfast. It tastes best with brown rice, which is far more nutritious than white, but it does need a little extra cooking time.

INGREDIENTS

10 ml (2 teaspoons) vegetable oil
60 g (2 oz) button mushrooms, wiped and sliced
1 spring onion, white only, finely chopped
60 g (2 oz) long-grain brown rice
300 ml (1/2 pint) vegetable stock
a pinch of ground turmeric
1 hard-boiled egg
1 tomato

1 Heat the oil in a saucepan and add the mushrooms and spring onion. Cook over a medium heat for 5 minutes. Stir in the rice and cook for 3–4 minutes, or until the rice is shiny. Add the stock and the turmeric and bring to the boil. Cover and simmer for 30 minutes, or until tender.

2 Shell the hard-boiled egg and cut it in wedges. Slice the tomato. Serve the kedgeree with the pieces of egg and tomato.

Honeydew refresher

Serves: *4*
Preparation time: *15 minutes*
Freezing: *not recommended*

Ingredients
1 honeydew melon
2 blood oranges
115 g (4 oz) seedless grapes, washed and dried
115 ml (4 fl oz) sparkling apple juice

A light mixture of melon, oranges and grapes that you can serve on its own with yogurt or make more substantial with cereal. It's high in vitamin C and natural sugar for energy and you can store it for up to two days in the fridge.

1 Halve the melon and scoop out the seeds. Cut the flesh in wedges, remove the skin and slice the flesh into a child's bite-size pieces. Put the pieces in a serving bowl.
2 Using a very sharp knife, peel oranges, holding the fruit over the bowl, and then carefully remove each segment. Halve the segments and add them to the bowl, with the grapes. Stir in the apple juice just before serving.

Swiss-style muesli

Serves: *1*
Preparation time: *5 minutes*
Freezing: *not recommended*

Ingredients
30 ml (2 tablespoons) muesli
60 ml (4 tablespoons) natural yogurt
60 ml (4 tablespoons) single cream

This has to be made the night before, so it is great for a frantic morning, when time is short. The oats and fruit in the muesli soften during soaking, resulting in a delicious, thick, creamy porridge, which the whole family will enjoy.

Spoon the muesli into a serving bowl and then stir in the yogurt and cream. Cover and chill overnight. Stir before serving.

Hints and tips
Use home-made muesli or an unsweetened commercial kind, but avoid those varieties that contain nuts, which will become unpleasantly soggy. Substitute fruit juice if your child cannot tolerate dairy products.

Alimoes

SERVES: *2*
PREPARATION TIME: *10 minutes*
COOKING TIME: *20 minutes*
FREEZING: *not recommended*

A breakfast based on sautéed potatoes with mushrooms and tomatoes, which my father used to make for me as a child. Use potatoes that have been cooked in their skins, for extra fibre and vitamin C.

INGREDIENTS
15 ml (1 tablespoon) corn oil
180 g (6 oz) cooked potato, cut in large chunks
60 g (2 oz) flat field mushrooms, wiped and sliced
1 beef tomato, cored and cut in wedges
5 ml (1 teaspoon) snipped fresh chives

1 Heat the oil in a non-stick frying pan. Add the potato and cook over a medium heat for 10 minutes, or until golden. Drain on kitchen paper and keep hot.
2 Add the mushrooms to the pan and cook for 5 minutes. Add the tomato wedges and cook for 3–4 minutes more, or until the mushrooms are tender and the tomatoes heated through.
3 Spoon the potato into a serving bowl and top with mushroom mixture. Sprinkle with the chives.

Bran tub

SERVES: *1*
PREPARATION TIME: *5 minutes*
FREEZING: *not recommended*

Add a surprise to breakfast time by putting a slice of fruit, a whole strawberry or a cherry in the base of your child's cereal dish. Children will eat quickly to reach the treat at the bottom in no time; it's a good way to encourage a "picky" eater.

INGREDIENTS
1 whole strawberry, stoned cherry, mandarin orange segment or a slice of your child's favourite fruit
150 g (5 oz) carton of Greek-style yogurt
15 ml (1 tablespoon) bran
15 ml (1 tablespoon) oatmeal, toasted
a pinch of demerara sugar

Place the fruit in the base of a clear tumbler or sundae dish. Layer the yogurt and the bran and oatmeal mixture in the dish, ending with a dollop of yogurt. Sprinkle with the demerara sugar before serving.

HINTS AND TIPS

Any breakfast cereal can be used with yogurt in this dish. Some children may prefer fruit yogurt.

LUNCHES

Often lunch is a child's main meal, so it must be substantial enough to provide at least a third of the daily nutritional requirements. All the recipes in this chapter have been designed with this requirement in mind. Tasty main-meal ideas, packed with the goodness of pulses, grains and vegetables, will satisfy the fussiest eaters.

Creamy corn pasta spirals

SERVES: *1*
PREPARATION TIME: *5 minutes*
COOKING TIME: *10 minutes*
FREEZING: *not recommended*

INGREDIENTS
5 ml (1 teaspoon) butter or margarine
1 small leek, trimmed, washed and finely sliced
60 g (2 oz) baby sweetcorn, washed and chopped
60 g (2 oz) frozen mixed peppers and peas
30 g (1 oz) canned red kidney beans, rinsed
5 ml (1 teaspoon) cornflour
150 ml (1/4 pint) milk
30 g (1 oz) three-coloured (tricolore) pasta spirals
15 g (1/2 oz) carrot, grated

A versatile sauce that can be spooned over jacket potatoes as well as served with pasta, as described here. The grated carrot topping adds vitamins A and C.

1 Melt the butter or margarine in a saucepan and cook the leek and sweetcorn for 5 minutes, or until tender. Stir in the peppers, peas and beans and cook for 2–3 minutes.
2 Mix the cornflour and milk together until smooth and then stir the mixture into the pan. Stir over a medium heat until the sauce thickens and is smooth. Simmer gently for a few minutes.
3 Meanwhile, cook the pasta in boiling water for 10 minutes, or as directed on the packet. Drain well. Spoon the pasta into a serving bowl and spoon over the sauce. Sprinkle the grated carrot on top before serving.

Vegetable lasagne

Children love pasta, but they often give vegetables the thumbs-down. If this is your problem, try disguising vegetables in this tasty package under a blanket of cheesy sauce.

SERVES: *2*
PREPARATION TIME: *20 minutes*
COOKING TIME: *1 hour 10 minutes*
FREEZING: *recommended*

INGREDIENTS
10 ml (2 teaspoons) sunflower oil
1/4 onion, finely chopped
85 g (3 oz) courgette, cut in tiny cubes
85 g (3 oz) carrot, cut in tiny cubes
60 g (2 oz) button mushrooms, wiped and quartered
1 strip each, red and green pepper, de-seeded and chopped
30 g (1 oz) frozen sweetcorn
60 ml (4 tablespoons) canned chopped tomatoes with herbs
10 ml (2 teaspoons) tomato ketchup
150 ml (1/4 pint) vegetable stock
FOR THE CHEESE SAUCE:
30 g (1 oz) butter or margarine
30 g (1 oz) unbleached plain flour
300 ml (1/2 pint) milk
45 g (1 1/2 oz) red Leicester cheese
a pinch of grated nutmeg
2 sheets of no-precook lasagne

1 Heat the oil in a saucepan and fry the onion for 5 minutes, or until softened. Add the remaining vegetables and cook for 5 minutes more. Stir in the tomatoes, tomato ketchup and stock. Bring the liquid to the boil and leave to simmer for 20 minutes. Preheat the oven to Gas Mark 4/180°C/350°F.
2 Meanwhile, to make the sauce, melt the butter or margarine in a clean pan. Add the flour and cook for 1 minute. Remove the pan from the heat and gradually stir in the milk. Stir over a medium heat until the sauce thickens and comes to the boil. Add half the cheese to the sauce and season with nutmeg.
3 Spoon half the vegetable mixture into the base of a 600 ml (1-pint) ovenproof dish. Top with a sheet of lasagne.
4 Spoon half the cheese sauce on top of the lasagne and then spoon on the remaining vegetable mixture. Place the second sheet of lasagne on top and then spoon over the remaining cheese sauce to cover the lasagne completely.
5 Sprinkle with the remaining cheese and cook in the oven for 35–40 minutes, or until the lasagne is tender and the top golden. Allow to cool slightly and then serve, with wedges of baby gem lettuce and tomato.

HINTS AND TIPS
If you like, make this in two 300 ml (1/2-pint) containers and freeze the second portion.

Southern-style rice and beans

SERVES: *2*
PREPARATION TIME: *15 minutes*
COOKING TIME: *35 minutes*
FREEZING: *not recommended*

INGREDIENTS
10 ml (2 teaspoons) corn oil
¼ onion, finely chopped
1 small garlic clove, crushed
1 strip each red and green pepper, de-seeded and chopped
60 g (2 oz) chestnut mushrooms, wiped and chopped
60 g (2 oz) long-grain white rice
60 ml (4 tablespoons) chopped canned tomatoes
300 ml (½ pint) vegetable stock
a pinch of dried marjoram
2.5 ml (½ teaspoon) corn or maple syrup
60 g (2 oz) green cabbage, shredded
30 g (1 oz) small frozen peas
30 g (1 oz) cooked red kidney beans

A hearty winter dish inspired by the rich bean stews of the southern states of the U.S.A. Children can easily eat this without help, because the rice sticks the other ingredients together as they are gathered on the spoon. Serve with carrot sticks.

1 Heat the oil in a saucepan and cook the onion and garlic for 5 minutes, or until softened. Stir in the peppers and mushrooms. Cook for 5 minutes. Add the rice, tomatoes, stock and marjoram. Bring to the boil.
2 Stir in the corn or maple syrup, cover and simmer for 15 minutes.
3 Add the cabbage, peas and kidney beans and return to the boil. Cook for 10 minutes, stirring occasionally.

Stir-fry with egg wheels

The egg wheels provide protein and calcium in this colourful stir-fry and they are no more difficult to make than an omelette. Serve with egg noodles, if your child likes them. Children enjoy the novelty of using grown-up china or cutlery, so if you have them, serve this in little Chinese bowls with Chinese-style spoons.

SERVES: *1*
PREPARATION TIME: *15 minutes*
COOKING TIME: *10 minutes*
FREEZING: *not recommended*

INGREDIENTS
1 size-3 egg
15 ml (1 tablespoon) low-sodium soy sauce
10 ml (2 teaspoons) groundnut oil
60 g (2 oz) carrot
60 g (2 oz) courgette
1 strip each yellow and red pepper, de-seeded and cut in matchsticks
30 g (1 oz) fresh bean sprouts, washed
30 g (1 oz) mange tout peas, trimmed and sliced
5 ml (1 teaspoon) sweet and sour stir-fry sauce

1 Beat the egg with the soy sauce. Heat half the oil in an 18 cm (7-inch) non-stick omelette pan. Add the egg and cook over a medium heat for 3 minutes, or until set. Flip the omelette over and cook the second side until golden.
2 Turn out the omelette on to a flat plate. When it's cool enough to handle, roll it up tightly like a swiss roll and reserve it for later.
3 Heat the remaining oil in the frying-pan and stir fry all the vegetables, except the bean sprouts and mange tout peas, for 4–5 minutes. Add the bean sprouts, peas and the stir-fry sauce and cook for 3 minutes.
3 Spoon the vegetables into a serving bowl. Slice the omelette into 1 cm (½-inch) wheels and arrange on top.

Barley pilaff

A pilaff is a Middle-Eastern dish consisting of lightly spiced vegetables with rice. It's usually made just with rice, but adding barley, which is rich in vitamins and minerals, adds interest and nutrition. Serve with cucumber and celery sticks.

SERVES: *2*
PREPARATION TIME: *15 minutes*
COOKING TIME: *35 minutes*
FREEZING: *not recommended*

INGREDIENTS
5 ml (1 teaspoon) olive oil
¼ small onion, finely chopped
1 x 1.75 ml (¼ teaspoon) ground cinnamon and ground coriander
30 g (1 oz) long-grain brown rice
45 g (1½ oz) pot barley
450 ml (¾ pint) vegetable stock
½ carrot, peeled and cut in sticks
½ courgette, cubed
30 g (1 oz) sultanas
30 g (1 oz) cooked chick-peas

1 Heat the oil in a saucepan and cook the onion over a medium heat until softened. Stir in the spices, rice and barley and cook until shiny.
2 Stir in the stock, carrot and courgette and bring to the boil. Reduce the heat, cover and simmer for 25 minutes.
3 Add the sultanas and chick-peas. Cook for 5 minutes, or until heated through.

Mixed bean and spinach pot

SERVES: *2*
PREPARATION TIME: *20 minutes*
COOKING TIME: *20 minutes*
FREEZING: *recommended*

INGREDIENTS

10 ml (2 teaspoons) olive oil
60 g (2 oz) each cooked red kidney beans, butter beans, chick-peas and flageolet beans
1 spring onion, trimmed and chopped
1 garlic clove, crushed
2 tomatoes, skinned and chopped
5 ml (1 teaspoon) tomato ketchup
30 g (1 oz) young spinach leaves, washed
225 g (8 oz) potato, peeled and chopped
30 ml (2 tablespoons) milk

A protein-rich main course that is also full of iron and potassium (which is necessary to balance and correct the body's water content). Smaller children may prefer the filling to be mashed. Serve with green beans.

1 Heat the oil in a saucepan and cook all the beans, the spring onion and the garlic over a medium heat for 4–5 minutes. Stir in the tomatoes and tomato ketchup and cook for 5 minutes more.
2 Meanwhile, put the spinach leaves into a clean pan and cook over a low heat, stirring frequently, until wilted. Remove the spinach, add the potatoes to the pan and cover them with cold water. Bring the water to the boil, reduce the heat and simmer for 15 minutes, or until tender. Drain the potatoes and mash them with the spinach and milk. Preheat the grill to hot.
3 Divide the bean mixture between two 300 ml (½-pint) heatproof dishes. Spoon the mashed potato and spinach mixture on top and cook under the grill until the topping is golden.

HINTS AND TIPS

For a richer version, stir some grated cheese into the topping and sprinkle over some more before grilling.

Sloppy joes

Soya mince is available ready-seasoned, so check you use the low-sodium (unseasoned) variety for children.

SERVES: *1*
PREPARATION TIME: *15 minutes*
COOKING TIME: *1 hour*
FREEZING: *recommended*

INGREDIENTS
180 g (6 oz) potato, scrubbed and cut in wedges
10 ml (2 teaspoons) corn oil
¼ onion, finely chopped
60 g (2 oz) carrot, grated
60 g (2 oz) parsnip, grated
115 g (4 oz) canned tomatoes
60 g (2 oz) soya mince
30 g (1 oz) frozen peas
5 ml (1 teaspoon) barbecue sauce

1 Preheat the oven to Gas Mark 6/200°C/400°F. Put the potatoes in a shallow dish and drizzle over 5 ml (1 teaspoon) of the oil. Cook the potatoes in the oven for 1 hour, or until they are golden. Turn the potatoes in the oil from time to time so they colour evenly all over.
2 Heat the remaining oil in a saucepan and cook the onion for 5 minutes, or until softened. Stir in remaining ingredients and bring to the boil. Simmer, stirring occasionally for 20 minutes, or until thickened and tender.
3 Arrange the potato wedges in a star pattern on a serving plate and spoon the mince mixture into the centre. Allow to cool slightly before serving.

Aubergine and lentil Bolognese

Vegetarian Bolognese sauces are among the best of vegetarian versions of classic dishes. Adults will enjoy this too.

SERVES: *2*
PREPARATION TIME: *20 minutes*
COOKING TIME: *30 minutes*
FREEZING: *not recommended*

INGREDIENTS
10 ml (2 teaspoons) sunflower oil
1 spring onion, trimmed and finely chopped
60 g (2 oz) aubergine, cubed finely
85 g (3 oz) carrot, cubed finely
1 strip each red and green pepper, de-seeded and chopped
30 g (1 oz) red lentils
60 ml (4 tablespoons) canned chopped tomatoes
115 ml (4 fl oz) vegetable stock
10 ml (2 teaspoons) tomato ketchup
a pinch of dried oregano
60 g (2 oz) spaghetti or pasta shapes
30 g (1 oz) Cheddar cheese, grated

1 Heat the oil in a saucepan and add the spring onion, aubergine, carrot and peppers. Cook over a medium heat for 10 minutes, or until softened. Stir in the lentils, tomatoes, stock and tomato ketchup. Bring to the boil. Sprinkle in the oregano, cover the pan and simmer for 20 minutes, or until the mixture has thickened slightly and the vegetables and lentils are tender.
2 Meanwhile, cook the pasta in a pan of boiling water for 10 minutes, or as directed on the packet. Drain well. If you are using spaghetti, chop it. Spoon the pasta into a serving dish and top it with the vegetable and lentil mixture. Sprinkle over the cheese just before serving.

SNACK LUNCHES

The recipes in this section are lighter than the main meals in the previous section, and many can be prepared in advance so you can produce something quickly when your child needs "topping up". If your child can't eat all they need from a main meal at one sitting, these recipes will be invaluable.

Rice baskets

SERVES: *2*
PREPARATION TIME: *15 minutes*
COOKING TIME: *20 minutes*
FREEZING: *recommended*

INGREDIENTS
1 small red pepper, halved lengthways and de-seeded
5 ml (1 teaspoon) sunflower oil
60 g (2 oz) button mushrooms, wiped and sliced
45 g (1½ oz) long-grain white rice
5 ml (1 teaspoon) smooth peanut butter
225 ml (8 fl oz) vegetable stock
60 g (2 oz) small broccoli florets
60 g (2 oz) cooked red kidney beans
30 g (1 oz) fresh or frozen sweetcorn

Colourful little baskets of rice and vegetables, these are overflowing with goodness. Your child may need help to cut up the pepper basket, once the filling has been eaten. Serve with a sesame breadstick.

1 Blanch the pepper halves in boiling water for 4 minutes, or until just tender. Drain well.
2 Heat the oil in a saucepan, add the mushrooms and cook for 3 minutes. Stir in the rice and peanut butter and cook over a medium heat for 1 minute. Pour over the stock and bring to the boil. Cover and simmer for 5 minutes.
3 Add the broccoli, kidney beans and sweetcorn and cook for a further 5 minutes, or until the rice is tender. Spoon the mixture equally between the pepper halves.

HINTS AND TIPS
The peppers will become soggy on freezing, so it's best to freeze the filling only.

Lightning burgers

MAKES: *6 burgers*
PREPARATION TIME: *30 minutes*
COOKING TIME: *20 minutes*
FREEZING: *recommended, after step 2*

So called because, once made, they disappear in a flash. Keep a batch handy, individually wrapped, in the freezer. They cook perfectly well from frozen. Serve in a toasted sesame bun, with frilly lettuce, sliced tomatoes, and relish. Cut in halves or quarters before serving to small children.

INGREDIENTS
340 g (12 oz) soya mince
1 small onion, grated
1 small carrot, grated
115 g (4 oz) wholemeal breadcrumbs
300 ml (½ pint) hot vegetable stock
1 size-3 egg
1.25 ml (¼ teaspoon) yeast extract

1 Mix together the soya mince, onion, carrot, and breadcrumbs. Stir in the stock. Leave to cool slightly and then add the egg and yeast extract. Leave until cold.
2 Using wetted hands, shape the mixture into six burgers, using a 7.5 cm (3-inch) plain pastry cutter as a guide. Put the burgers on a baking sheet and chill until required.
3 Cook under a preheated grill or lightly fry for 10 minutes, turning once, until cooked through.

Vegetable crunchies

MAKES: *8 crunchies*
PREPARATION TIME: *25 minutes*
COOKING TIME: *15 minutes*
FREEZING: *recommended*

Smooth peanut butter adds protein and helps to bind the ingredients together in these tasty fingers. Serve with spaghetti hoops in tomato sauce.

INGREDIENTS
340 g (12 oz) potato, peeled and cut in chunks
60 g (2 oz) frozen special mixed vegetables
1 spring onion, trimmed and finely chopped
15 ml (1 tablespoon) smooth peanut butter
30 ml (2 tablespoons) milk
1 size-3 egg
60 g (2 oz) white breadcrumbs
30 g (1 oz) finely grated red Leicester cheese
5 ml (1 teaspoon) sesame seeds
oil for shallow-frying

1 Cook the potatoes in boiling water for 10 minutes. Add the mixed vegetables and spring onion and cook for 5 minutes. Drain well.
2 Remove the potatoes and mash them with the peanut butter and milk, until smooth. Stir in the vegetables and leave until cold.
3 Beat the egg on a plate. On a separate plate, mix together the breadcrumbs, cheese and sesame seeds. Divide the vegetable mixture into eight equal portions. Shape into small finger-length rectangles.
4 Coat each finger in egg and then in the crumb mixture. Chill until required.
5 Heat about 15 ml (1 tablespoon) of oil in a non-stick frying-pan and cook the vegetable crunchies for 8 minutes, turning once, until golden. Drain on kitchen paper.

Mimosa eggs

SERVES: *1*
PREPARATION TIME: *5 minutes*
FREEZING: *not recommended*

INGREDIENTS
1 hard-boiled egg
5 ml (1 teaspoon) mayonnaise
5 ml (1 teaspoon) natural yogurt
30 g (1 oz) carrot, grated
5 ml (1 teaspoon) raisins
2 lettuce leaves
alfalfa sprouts
2 cherry tomatoes, quartered
2 stuffed olives, sliced

Hard-boiled eggs are a great convenience food and a cheap source of protein. The whites are ideal containers for all manner of delicious fillings, but the yolks are high in cholesterol, so limit your child's consumption of eggs to about four a week. Serve with a granary bap.

1 Halve the egg and mash the yolk in a small bowl, with the mayonnaise and yogurt. Stir in the carrot and raisins.
2 Arrange the lettuce leaves and alfalfa sprouts on a plate. Spoon the egg-yolk filling back into the egg whites. Place the egg-halves on top of the lettuce. Arrange the tomatoes and olives on top and serve immediately.

Spring rolls

MAKES: *12 rolls*
PREPARATION TIME: *20 minutes*
COOKING TIME: *15 minutes*
FREEZING: *recommended*

INGREDIENTS
½ carrot, cut in matchsticks
½ small red or green pepper, de-seeded and cut in tiny cubes
6 mange tout peas, shredded
30 g (1 oz) fresh bean sprouts
85 g (3 oz) tofu, cut in small cubes
5 ml (1 teaspoon) tomato ketchup
15 ml (1 tablespoon) low-sodium soy sauce
6 spring-roll wrappers
groundnut oil for frying

You'll find ready-made spring-roll wrappers in the supermarket's freezer section; alternatively, use filo or thinly rolled flaky pastry. Serve with soy sauce for dipping, and carrot and cucumber sticks.

1 Mix the vegetables and tofu together in a bowl. Stir in the tomato ketchup and soy sauce and leave to soak for about 30 minutes.
2 Halve each spring-roll wrapper and moisten the edge with water. Divide the filling between each wrapper and roll them up, tucking in the ends to seal the roll like a parcel.
3 Heat the oil in a shallow frying-pan until a cube of bread will sizzle within 30 seconds. Fry half the spring rolls over a medium heat for about 8 minutes, or until golden. Drain on kitchen paper and keep hot while frying the second batch.

HINTS AND TIPS
Open-freeze uncooked spring rolls until firm and then wrap them in freezer film.

Tomato and spinach pie

This colourful, layered dish couldn't be simpler. Make it in one large or four small ramekins. Serve with vegetable sticks.

SERVES: *4*
PREPARATION TIME: *30 minutes*
COOKING TIME: *1 hour*
FREEZING: *not recommended*

INGREDIENTS

225 g (8 oz) fresh young spinach leaves, rinsed and shredded
60 g (2 oz) Cheddar cheese, grated
4 firm tomatoes, thinly sliced
3 potatoes, peeled and thinly sliced
2 size-3 eggs
450 ml (¾ pint) milk

1 Preheat the oven to Gas Mark 5/190°C/375°F. Cook the spinach in a saucepan over a medium heat for 5 minutes, or until wilted. Press the spinach in a sieve to remove excess water.
2 Lightly oil four 180 ml (6 fl oz) ramekins or a 15-cm (6-inch) soufflé dish. Layer up the Cheddar cheese, tomatoes, spinach and potatoes, ending with a layer of potatoes.
3 Beat the eggs and milk together and then pour them over the vegetables in the dish(es). Cover with foil and bake for 1 hour, or until the potatoes are tender and the custard set.
4 Allow to cool for a few minutes in the dish and then turn the pie out on to the plate.

Peanut powerballs

Peanuts pack an awful lot of protein into a small nut, but they need to be combined with other protein-rich foods to provide all the necessary amino acids. Soya meal provides just that. Serve with tomato wedges and oven chips.

MAKES: *8 powerballs*
PREPARATION TIME: *20 minutes*
COOKING TIME: *35 minutes*
FREEZING: *recommended*

INGREDIENTS

10 ml (2 teaspoons) sunflower oil
½ small onion, peeled and finely chopped
1 celery stick, finely chopped
1 carrot, finely cubed
1 strip each red and green pepper, de-seeded and chopped
60 g (2 oz) green beans, trimmed and sliced
5 ml (1 teaspoon) tomato ketchup
60 g (2 oz) unsalted peanuts
60 g (2 oz) cooked brown rice
1 size-3 egg, beaten
85 g (3 oz) wholemeal breadcrumbs
30 g (1 oz) soya meal

1 Heat the oil in a saucepan and cook the vegetables for 5 minutes. Stir in the tomato ketchup, cover and cook over a low heat for 10 minutes, or until tender.
2 Blend the peanuts in a food processor until smooth. Add the cooked vegetables and rice, and blend briefly until finely chopped. Stir in half the egg and 30 g (1 oz) of the breadcrumbs.
3 Using wetted hands, shape the mixture into eight small balls. Coat the balls in soya meal, dip them in the remaining egg and then roll them in the remaining breadcrumbs. Chill until required.
4 Preheat the oven to Gas Mark 7/220°C/425°F. Put the powerballs on a baking sheet and cook them for 20 minutes, or until crisp and golden.

LUNCH BOXES

Giving children their own lunch boxes enables you to keep control of their eating, provided, of course, that they don't swap with their friends! In this section both sweet and savoury recipe ideas are provided. Try to include a high-protein and energy combination every day, plus a fruit-juice drink, a piece of fruit or a fruit yogurt.

Sandwiches

The ubiquitous sandwich can be made up with an infinite variety of fillings. Here I have included some of my family's favourites, plus some novel ideas of how to ring the changes from the usual squares or triangles.

Presentation is very important to a child. You'll soon discover they eat most of what they find attractive. Fortunately, sandwiches can come in all shapes, colours and sizes.

▲Try using different types of bread: pitta bread, ciabatta, dried fruit bread, nut loaves, rolls, bagels, French bread, English muffins, naan bread or tortillas.

▲Use cutters to shape sliced bread into little people, a favourite animal (cats and dogs always seem popular), cars, boats, trains, trucks or any other shape.

▲Make pinwheel sandwiches, by trimming the crusts from thinly sliced bread. Roll them to flatten them and then spread the slices with the filling. Roll the bread up and slice into wheels.

▲Make checkerboard sandwiches by using 1 white and 1 brown slice of bread. Cut off the crusts and cut the sandwiches in 2.5 cm (1-inch) squares and then fit the squares back together in a checker-board pattern, alternating brown and white squares.

▲Make spotty sandwiches by using the end of a piping nozzle to remove 1 cm (½-inch) discs from 1 white and 1 brown slice of bread. Replace the white discs in the holes in the brown bread and vice versa.

▲Make open sandwiches by toasting one side of a slice of bread and topping it with filling.

▲More elaborate open sandwiches can be made by trimming away the crusts from a slice of bread and rolling the slice to flatten it somewhat. Spoon the filling diagonally across the centre and then lift up opposite corners, pinch them together and fasten them together with a matchstick of carrot or cucumber.

HINTS AND TIPS

Wrap sandwiches in non-PVC cling film or foil, or put them in a plastic sandwich carton before packing the lunch box, to keep the sandwiches fresh. During hot weather, include a small, frozen picnic block in the lunchbox.

SANDWICH FILLINGS

We would need a whole book to cover all the possibilities, but here is my top twenty.

Mashed avocado, lemon juice and cottage cheese

Mashed avocado, lemon juice, and frilly lettuce

Mashed banana and date spread

Mashed banana and smooth peanut butter

Cream cheese, toasted sesame seeds and cress

Cream cheese, toasted ground walnuts and watercress

Cream cheese and chopped dried apricots

Grated Cheddar cheese and chopped mango chutney

Grated Cheddar cheese, tomato and corn relish

Grated Cheddar cheese, grated apple and sultanas

Grated Cheddar cheese and coleslaw

Hard-boiled egg, mashed with mayonnaise, yogurt and a pinch of curry powder

Hard-boiled egg, mashed with mayonnaise, and cucumber

Hard-boiled egg, mashed with mayonnaise and yogurt, and alfalfa sprouts

Chopped falafel with hummus and tomato

Sliced falafel with grated carrot, sesame seeds and raisins

Hummus, shredded carrot and sliced cucumber

Yeast extract and scrambled eggs

Smoked tofu and barbecue sauce

Smoked tofu, sliced tomato and tomato chutney

MAKES: *4 pasties*
PREPARATION TIME: *15 minutes*
CHILLING TIME: *15 minutes*
COOKING TIME: *20 minutes*
FREEZING: *not recommended*

INGREDIENTS
115 g (4 oz) unbleached white flour
115 g (4 oz) wholemeal flour
115 g (4 oz) margarine
200 g can of baked beans in tomato sauce
60 g (2 oz) each cooked borlotti and red kidney beans
1 celery stick, trimmed and finely chopped
15 ml (1 tablespoon) chopped fresh coriander
a pinch of ground cumin
a little milk
5 ml (1 teaspoon) black poppy seeds

Cheesy bean pasties

If you have a pastry press, these can be shaped in no time; if not, use a saucer or pastry cutter as a guide for cutting out the pastry circles.

1 Sift the flours into a bowl and return any bran left in the sieve to the bowl. Rub the margarine into the flours until the mixture resembles fine breadcrumbs. Stir in enough water to form a soft, but not sticky, ball of dough.
2 Roll out the dough on a lightly floured surface. Cut out four 13-cm (5-inch) circles and moisten the edges. Mix together the beans, celery, coriander and cumin. Spoon an equal portion of filling into the centre of each circle.
3 Lift the edges of the dough and press the edges together to seal. Put the pasties on a baking sheet, spaced a little apart, and chill them for 15 minutes. Meanwhile, preheat the oven to Gas Mark 6/200°C/400°F.
4 Brush the top of each pasty with milk and then sprinkle over the poppy seeds. Bake the pasties for 20 minutes or until the pastry is golden.

MAKES: *6 large muffins or 12 mini-muffins*
PREPARATION TIME: *10 minutes*
COOKING TIME: *25 minutes for large muffins; 15 minutes for mini-muffins*
FREEZING: *not recommended*

INGREDIENTS
285 g (10 oz) unbleached plain flour
15 ml (1 tablespoon) baking powder
A pinch of salt
2 size-3 eggs
225 ml (8 fl oz) milk
115 g (4 oz) butter or margarine, melted

Mighty muffins

These can be sweet or savoury, with as simple or complex a filling as you want. I prefer them made with unbleached white flour, but for more fibre, calcium and vitamin B, make them with wholemeal flour or use a mixture of the two.

1 Preheat the oven to Gas Mark 6/200°C/400°F. Grease the muffin tin with oil. Sift the flour, baking powder and salt together. In a large bowl, beat together the eggs, milk and melted butter or margarine. Sift in the dry ingredients.
2 Mix together gently; do not over-beat. Add your chosen flavouring and mix in lightly. Spoon into the tin and cook for 20–25 minutes for large muffins, 15 minutes for mini-muffins. Cool on a wire rack.

SAVOURY VARIATIONS:

Cheese and onion muffins
Fry ½ finely chopped onion in oil until golden. Allow to cool and then add to the muffin mixture with 60 g (2 oz) of grated Cheddar cheese. Top with extra grated cheese before baking.

Sunshine seeds muffins
Add 30 g (1 oz) of sunflower seeds and 2.5 ml (½ teaspoon) of yeast extract to the muffin mixture. Sprinkle the muffins with sesame seeds before baking.

Peanut muffins
Stir 30 ml (2 tablespoons) of smooth peanut butter into the muffin mixture.

Carrot and mustard muffins
Grate 1 medium carrot and stir it into the muffin mixture, with 10 ml (2 teaspoons) of coarse-grain mustard.

SWEET VARIATIONS:

Add 85 g (3 oz) of caster sugar and 5 ml (1 teaspoon) of vanilla extract to the melted mixture in all cases.

Chocolate and raisin muffins
Roughly chop 85 g (3 oz) of plain or milk chocolate and stir into the muffin mixture, with 45 g (1½ oz) of raisins.

Carrot and orange muffins
Grate 1 carrot and add it to the muffin mixture, with the grated zest of 1 unwaxed orange. Top with a sprinkling of preserving sugar crystals.

Cherry and lemon muffins
Add 85 g (3 oz) of chopped glacé cherries and the grated zest of 1 small unwaxed lemon to the muffin mixture. Top with 30 g (1 oz) of chopped glacé cherries.

Salad servings

A sneaky way to get your children to eat more greenery and fibre is to give them their own lunch-pot of salad. Make it up in layers, rather like a savoury knickerbocker glory. That way they won't be bored by one taste or texture. Choose from the following:

New-potato and chive salad
Scrub new potatoes and cook them in their skins. While they are still warm, toss them in a mixture of mayonnaise, yogurt, and snipped chives.

Spinach and crispy bread salad
Fry cubes of bread in olive oil until crisp. Drain on kitchen paper. While still warm, toss with washed and dried young spinach leaves, halved cherry tomatoes and cubed cucumber.

Sprouting salad
Cube silken tofu and toss the cubes with fresh bean sprouts, grated carrot and alfalfa sprouts. Finely chop some cucumber and add it, with a dressing made with low-sodium soy sauce, sesame oil and fresh orange juice.

Pink ink salad
Mix together cream cheese, mayonnaise, chopped hard-boiled egg, and finely cubed cooked beetroot.

Cheese and pineapple salad
Cube Cheddar cheese and mix it with fresh or canned pineapple pieces, cottage cheese and a little yogurt.

Nuts and bolts salad
Mix together cooked red kidney beans, black-eyed beans, haricot beans and sweetcorn. Cube some cucumber and stir it in, with some watercress. Toss in a little vinaigrette dressing.

Flapjack fingers

MAKES: *10 flapjacks*
PREPARATION TIME: *5 minutes*
COOKING TIME: *20 minutes*
FREEZING: *not recommended*

Bar biscuits have become increasingly popular in the last few years, and they take so little effort to make that it is really worthwhile to make your own.

INGREDIENTS
85 g (3 oz) block margarine
60 g (2 oz) light muscovado sugar
30 ml (2 tablespoons) golden syrup
185 g (6 oz) rolled oats
5 ml (1 teaspoon) vanilla extract

1 Lightly grease an 18-cm (7-inch) square shallow tin. Preheat the oven to Gas Mark 4/180°C/350°F. Melt the margarine in a saucepan with the sugar and syrup.
2 Add the oats and vanilla extract and stir well to coat. Spoon into the tin, pressing it down well with the back of a spoon. Cook for 20 minutes, or until golden.
3 Allow to cool slightly in the tin and then mark into fingers and loosen the edges. When cold, remove from tin and break into fingers. Store the flapjacks in an airtight container for up to a week. (They probably won't last that long!)

Mushroom rolls

MAKES: *12 rolls*
PREPARATION TIME: *35 minutes*
CHILLING TIME: *15 minutes*
COOKING TIME: *30 minutes*
FREEZING: *recommended*

These look just like sausage rolls and are made in the same way, but they are much healthier and more tasty.

INGREDIENTS
225 g (8 oz) wholemeal flour
115 g (4 oz) margarine
FOR THE FILLING:
15 ml (1 tablespoon) olive oil
1 garlic clove, crushed
450 g (1 lb) button mushrooms, wiped and finely chopped
a pinch of ground coriander
15 ml (1 tablespoon) chopped fresh parsley
115 g (4 oz) wholemeal breadcrumbs
1 size-3 egg, beaten
10 ml (2 teaspoons) sesame seeds

1 Sift the flour into a bowl and return any bran left in the sieve to the bowl. Rub the margarine into the flour until the mixture resembles fine breadcrumbs. Add enough cold water to make a soft, but not sticky, ball of dough. Wrap and chill until required.
2 Heat the olive oil in a saucepan and add the garlic and mushrooms. Cook over a medium heat for 10 minutes, stirring frequently until tender. Spoon into a blender or a food processor and blend with the coriander, parsley and breadcrumbs. Stir in enough egg to bind.
3 Roll out the dough on a lightly floured surface to a 30 x 20 cm (12 x 8 inch) rectangle. Halve lengthways. Divide the filling in half and spoon half down the centre of each portion of dough. Moisten the edges with water and lift the edges over the filling. Press the edges together to seal them.
4 Cut into 5 cm (2-inch) rolls. Place the rolls on a baking sheet spaced a little apart. Chill for 15 minutes. Preheat the oven to Gas Mark 6/200°C/400°F. Brush the rolls with milk and sprinkle them with sesame seeds. Bake for 15–20 minutes, or until golden.

SIDE DISHES

Simple meals can be enhanced by the addition of imaginative and complementary side dishes. They don't need to be complicated and time-consuming to prepare, and they can often be a clever way to serve vegetables appealingly (or even incognito!), to children who aren't keen on vegetables. There are creative ideas for presenting faithful old spuds, and entertaining ways to present nutritious but not always popular vegetables like carrots, cabbage and spinach.

Sesame spuds

SERVES: *4*
PREPARATION TIME: *15 minutes*
COOKING TIME: *1 hour*
FREEZING: *not recommended*

INGREDIENTS
450 g (1 lb) potatoes
60 ml (4 tablespoons) corn oil
10 ml (2 teaspoons) sesame oil
15 ml (1 tablespoon) sesame seeds

HINTS AND TIPS
Cook sweet potatoes in the same way. Allow the potatoes to cool slightly before serving to small children.

Children love the crunchy texture of these roasted potatoes. They are great with salads, or serve them as an alternative to baked jacket potatoes.

1 Peel the potatoes and cut them in wedges. Using a sharp knife, make slits along one side, taking care not to cut right through. Put the potatoes in a saucepan and cover them with cold water. Bring the water to the boil and cook for about 10 minutes, or until tender.
2 Meanwhile, preheat the oven to Gas Mark 6/200°C/400°F. Put the corn and sesame oils into an ovenproof shallow dish. Heat the dish in the oven for 5 minutes.
3 Drain the potatoes and add them to the dish. Toss them well to coat them in the oil. Return to the oven and cook for 30 minutes. Sprinkle with the sesame seeds and cook for a further 30 minutes, or until the potatoes are crisp and golden. Drain on kitchen paper and serve straight away.

Rösti potatoes

MAKES: *10 potato cakes*
PREPARATION TIME: *10 minutes*
COOKING TIME: *20 minutes*
FREEZING: *not recommended*

Less fatty than deep-fried potatoes, these little lacy potato cakes are delicious. Cook them in a bland-tasting oil, such as corn or sunflower oil.

INGREDIENTS
225 g (8 oz) potato
oil for shallow-frying

1 Peel and coarsely grate the potato. Rinse well in a sieve until the water runs clear and then press dry in a clean tea towel.
2 Heat the oil in a large frying-pan. Take about 30 ml (2 tablespoons) potato and put in the pan, in a little cluster. Press down slightly with the back of a fish slice.
3 Repeat to make about five potato cakes. Cook over a medium heat for about 5 minutes, or until the underside is golden. Flip the cakes over and cook the second sides. Drain on kitchen paper and keep hot.
4 Cook the second batch in the same way. Serve immediately.

HINTS AND TIPS
Make a mixed vegetable rösti by grating a carrot, onion or courgette. Mix with the potato and cook as described above.

Stuffed tomatoes

SERVES: *2*
PREPARATION TIME: *10 minutes*
FREEZING: *not recommended*

These can be prepared in advance and are very popular, because they can be eaten just with a spoon.

INGREDIENTS
1 large beef tomato or 2 small tomatoes
1 hard-boiled egg, shelled and roughly chopped
30 g (1 oz) special mixed vegetables, cooked
15 ml (1 tablespoon) mayonnaise
5 ml (1 teaspoon) yogurt
a few snipped fresh chives

1 Halve the tomato(es). Carefully scoop out flesh and discard the seeds. Put the chopped egg in a bowl with the tomato flesh, vegetables, mayonnaise and yogurt. Mix well.
2 Spoon the filling back in the tomato shells and sprinkle with snipped chives.

HINTS AND TIPS
Transform these into boats by making a mast from a stick of carrot and sails from a slice of cheese.

Fried rice

SERVES: *2*
PREPARATION TIME: *5 minutes*
COOKING TIME: *12 minutes*
FREEZING: *not recommended*

INGREDIENTS
45 g (1½ oz) long-grain white rice
30 g (1 oz) small frozen peas
30 g (1 oz) frozen sweetcorn
1 strip red pepper, de-seeded and cubed
5 ml (1 teaspoon) sesame oil
10 ml (2 teaspoons) low-sodium light soy sauce
1 size-3 egg

As rice is often a child's first food, it is not surprising how popular it becomes. Add some cooked kidney beans or extra vegetables to turn this simple side dish into a main-course meal.

1 Cook the rice in boiling water for 5 minutes. Add the peas, sweetcorn and pepper and return to the boil. Cook for a further 5 minutes, or until the rice and vegetables are tender. Drain the rice and vegetables well.
2 Rinse and dry the pan. Add the oil and heat it gently. Beat the soy sauce with the egg. Return the rice mixture to the pan, and, stirring continuously, add the egg.
3 Cook over a high heat, stirring, until the egg has set completely. Serve immediately.

Vegetable fritters

SERVES: *4*
PREPARATION TIME: *10 minutes*
COOKING TIME: *10 minutes*
FREEZING: *not recommended*

INGREDIENTS
115 g (4 oz) unbleached plain flour
15 ml (1 tablespoon) cornflour
2 egg whites, whisked lightly
15 ml (1 tablespoon) low-sodium light soy sauce
groundnut oil for deep-frying
4 button mushrooms, wiped
1 courgette, cut in 1 cm (½-inch) pieces
5 cm (2-inch) piece of aubergine, cut in small cubes
4 broccoli florets
2 tomatoes, cut in wedges

Another great way for children to enjoy the natural taste of vegetables is in this light batter. They are deep-fried for only a few minutes, and retain all their goodness and flavour.

1 Mix the flours together in a bowl. Make a well in the centre and add the egg whites, soy sauce and enough water to give the consistency of double cream. Leave to stand for a few minutes.
2 Meanwhile, heat the oil in a deep pan until the temperature reaches 190°C/375°F, or when a cube of bread rises and sizzles within 30 seconds.
3 Meanwhile, add the vegetables to the batter. Mix lightly to coat the vegetables completely. Deep-fry the mushrooms and courgettes for 2–3 minutes, or until golden. Drain on kitchen paper. Then cook the aubergine and broccoli for about the same time. Finally, cook the tomatoes for 1–2 minutes only.

Glazed carrots

Old carrots contain more vitamin A than young ones, and what better way to use them up but in this tasty dish?

SERVES: *2*
PREPARATION TIME: *5 minutes*
COOKING TIME: *10 minutes*
FREEZING: *not recommended*

INGREDIENTS
1 large carrot, cut in sticks
15 g ($\frac{1}{2}$ oz) butter or margarine
grated zest and juice of 1 small unwaxed orange
5 ml (1 teaspoon) demerara sugar

1 Put the carrots, butter or margarine, orange zest and juice and sugar in a medium-size saucepan and cook over a low heat until the butter or margarine has melted.
2 Cook uncovered, stirring occasionally, for 10 minutes, or until the carrots are tender and the liquid has more or less evaporated. Sprinkle with parsley before serving.

Ratatouille

The aubergines and courgette are salted to get rid of their bitter juices. Take care to rinse them well before you cook them, especially if you are serving this to a child under three years old.

SERVES: *6*
PREPARATION TIME: *20 minutes*
STANDING TIME: *30 minutes*
COOKING TIME: *1 hour*
FREEZING: *recommended*

INGREDIENTS
1 aubergine
2 courgettes
10 ml (2 teaspoons) salt
15 ml (1 tablespoon) olive oil
1 small onion, finely chopped
1 small garlic clove, crushed
1 each, small green and red pepper, de-seeded and chopped
450 g (1 lb) tomatoes, skinned, de-seeded and chopped
15 ml (1 tablespoon) tomato purée
a pinch of dried mixed herbs
a pinch of soft brown sugar

1 Trim the aubergine and courgettes. Cut them in a child's bite-size cubes and layer them in a colander, set over a plate, with salt. Leave for 30 minutes.
2 Preheat the oven to Gas Mark 4/180°C/350°F. Rinse the aubergine and courgettes thoroughly and then dry them with kitchen paper. Heat the oil in a flameproof casserole and cook the onion and garlic for 5 minutes, or until softened. Add all the other vegetables and cook over a medium heat for 10 minutes, stirring occasionally.
3 Stir in the tomato purée, herbs and sugar. Cover and cook in the oven for 1 hour, or until the vegetables are tender.

HINTS AND TIPS

For a main meal, top with 115 g (4 oz) breadcrumbs, mixed with grated cheese. Grill until golden.

Home-baked beans

SERVES: *10*
SOAKING TIME: *overnight*
PREPARATION TIME: *20 minutes*
COOKING TIME: *3½ hours*
FREEZING: *recommended*

INGREDIENTS
225 g (8 oz) dried haricot beans
450 g (1 lb) tomatoes, skinned and de-seeded
30 ml (2 tablespoons) tomato purée
30 ml (2 tablespoons) molasses
10 ml (2 teaspoons) mustard powder
400 ml (¾ pint) hot vegetable stock

HINTS AND TIPS
Freeze single portions in empty yogurt pots.

Home-made baked beans bear no resemblance to the commercial canned variety. The long, slow cooking intensifies the flavour without ruining their nutritional quality. The beans are high in protein, calcium, iron and potassium.

1 Put the beans in a large bowl and cover with cold water. Leave to soak overnight.
2 Drain the beans well. Put them in a saucepan and cover with cold water by at least 5 cm (2 inches). Bring the water to the boil. Skim the surface, cover the pan and cook at a rolling boil for about 25 minutes. Drain well.
3 Preheat the oven to Gas Mark 2/150°C/300°F. Put the beans in a large casserole and stir in the tomatoes. Mix together the tomato purée, molasses, mustard and stock. Pour the stock mixture over the beans and mix well.
4 Cover the casserole and cook the beans for 2½ hours. Stir gently and cook for a further 35 minutes, or until the beans are tender and the sauce thickened. Serve hot or cold.

Popeye's spinach

SERVES: *8*
PREPARATION TIME: *20 minutes*
COOKING TIME: *10 minutes*
FREEZING: *recommended*

INGREDIENTS
900 g (2 lb) fresh spinach leaves, washed
2 spring onions, trimmed and finely chopped
30 g (1 oz) butter or margarine
115 ml (4 fl oz) single cream
a pinch of ground nutmeg

Spinach is available all year round and it contains a good quantity of iron and vitamin C. The young leaves are best served raw in salads, but this cooked dish adds protein, energy and vitamin D.

1 Put the spinach leaves in a large saucepan, with the spring onions and butter or margarine. Cook over a medium heat for 10 minutes, or until tender, stirring frequently. Drain well.
2 Return the spinach to the pan and stir in the cream and nutmeg. Reheat gently, stirring. Serve at once.

Crunchy seaweed

Truth to tell, this is not seaweed but finely shredded green cabbage. When prepared in this way, however, cabbage makes great imitation seaweed and this is what most Chinese restaurants serve. Children love the idea that they are eating sea greens.

SERVES: *4*
PREPARATION TIME: *5 minutes*
COOKING TIME: *5 minutes*
FREEZING: *not recommended*

INGREDIENTS
115 g (4 oz) dark green cabbage, finely shredded
groundnut oil for deep-frying
5 ml (1 teaspoon) granulated sugar
2.5 ml (½ teaspoon) sea salt

1 Rinse the cabbage and dry it thoroughly in a salad spinner or clean tea towel. Heat the oil in a deep frying-pan until the temperature reaches 190°C/375°F, or when a cube of bread rises to the surface and starts to sizzle within 30 seconds of being dropped in the oil.
2 Add the cabbage and stir gently, so that all the leaves are immersed. Cook for 2 minutes.
3 Meanwhile, mix the sugar and salt together. Drain the cabbage on kitchen paper and sprinkle it with the seasoning mixture immediately. Serve as soon as possible.

HINTS AND TIPS
Serve this with oriental-style meals, such as stir-fries or spring rolls.

Coleslaw

Most children like coleslaw, and a good job too, because coleslaw has a generous provision of vitamins and fibre; however it is low in protein, so serve it with something else to balance the meal. For variety, and to boost the nutrients, try adding cubes of cheese, cooked red kidney beans, dried apricots, sultanas or grated apple.

SERVES: *6*
PREPARATION TIME: *10 minutes*
FREEZING: *not recommended*

INGREDIENTS
¼ white cabbage, finely shredded
1 carrot, finely shredded
½ small onion, finely shredded
1 celery stick, finely chopped
15 ml (1 tablespoon) chopped fresh parsley
115 g (4 fl oz) mayonnaise
60 ml (4 tablespoons) yogurt
salt and pepper

Mix all the ingredients together in a bowl. Cover and chill for 2 hours, or until required.

HINTS AND TIPS
Unlike commercially-made coleslaw, this will not keep for more than 2 days in the fridge.

PUDDINGS

When you have a family to feed, puddings have to be quick, easy and nutritious. So here you'll find a number of ideas – from prepare-ahead puddings that can be cooked alongside the main-course dish to quick refrigerator puddings – as well as some classic favourites that, with a little adjustment, can easily fit into the healthy-eating style of today.

Bread and butter pudding

SERVES: *4*
PREPARATION TIME: *10 minutes*
SOAKING TIME: *30 minutes*
COOKING TIME: *1 hour*
FREEZING: *not recommended*

INGREDIENTS
6 slices of malted whole-grain bread
60 g (2 oz) butter or margarine
60 g (2 oz) mixed dried fruit, e.g., figs, apricots, peaches, raisins, currants, etc.
45 g (1½ oz) soft light brown sugar
2 size-3 eggs
600 ml (1 pint) milk

A great nursery pudding that never seems to date. This is the ideal "afters" to have ready on cold winter days, when the children arrive home ravenous after games. Its high protein, carbohydrate, and calcium content will certainly help to replace the energy lost on a frozen sports field.

1 Lightly grease a 1.1-litre (2-pint) ovenproof dish. Spread the slices of bread with the butter or margarine and cut them into triangles. Layer them in the dish, with the dried fruit and sugar.
2 Beat the eggs and milk together and pour them over the bread. Leave to soak for 30 minutes. Preheat the oven to Gas Mark 3/170°C/325°F.
3 Bake for 45 minutes to 1 hour, or until set and golden.

HINTS AND TIPS

Schoolchildren love this topped with a spoonful of jam. A less sweet alternative is to use a fruit spread instead of jam.

Knights, castles and custard

A simple steamed pudding that can be left to cook itself. Traditionally this is made with a red-fruit jam; to reduce the sugar, choose a low-sugar fruit spread instead. Serve with custard.

1 Grease and line the base of four individual pudding basins or teacups. Using an electric whisk, beat together the margarine, sugar, flour and eggs, until smooth.

2 Divide the fruit spread equally between the basins and then spoon in the batter. Cover the tops with foil and steam for 1¼ hours, or until the puddings have risen and a fine skewer comes out clean when you insert it.

3 To make the custard: beat the egg yolks, sugar, cornflour and vanilla extract together. Heat the milk and then pour it into the egg mixture. Return to the pan and stir over a low heat until the mixture just coats the back of a spoon.

4 Loosen the edges of the puddings and then turn them out into serving bowls. Allow to cool slightly before serving to "tinies".

SERVES: *4*
PREPARATION TIME: *15 minutes*
COOKING TIME: *1¼ hours*
FREEZING: *recommended*

INGREDIENTS
115 g (4 oz) soft margarine
115 g (4 oz) caster sugar
115 g (4 oz) unbleached plain flour
2 size-3 eggs
60 ml (4 tablespoons) red-fruit spread
FOR THE CUSTARD:
2 egg yolks
15 ml (1 tablespoon) caster sugar
15 ml (1 tablespoon) cornflour
5 ml (1 teaspoon) vanilla extract
400 ml (¾ pint) milk

Rice and sultana pudding

To be at its best, this does need long, slow cooking, but the preparation takes almost no time at all. It is a high-energy and high-protein pudding, ideal for cold wintry days.

Preheat the oven to Gas Mark 2/150°C/300°F. Put the rice, sugar and sultanas into a 900 ml (1½-pint) ovenproof dish. Stir in the milk, and then float the butter or margarine on top. Sprinkle with the nutmeg and cook for 2 hours, or until the rice is tender and the top golden.

SERVES: *4*
PREPARATION TIME: *2 minutes*
COOKING TIME: *2 hours*
FREEZING: *not recommended*

INGREDIENTS
60 g (2 oz) short-grain white rice
60 g (2 oz) light soft brown sugar
60 g (2 oz) sultanas
600 ml (1 pint) milk
30 g (1 oz) butter or margarine
a pinch of grated nutmeg

HINTS AND TIPS
For added fibre, serve this with sliced banana.

Toffee creams

SERVES: *6*
PREPARATION TIME: *15 minutes*
COOKING TIME: *1¼ hours*
CHILLING TIME: *overnight*
FREEZING: *recommended*

INGREDIENTS
115 g (4 oz) granulated sugar
150 ml (¼ pint) cold water
4 size-3 eggs
600 ml (1 pint) milk
2.5 ml (½ teaspoon) vanilla extract

HINTS AND TIPS
Remove from the fridge 30 minutes before serving.

This, as you would expect, contains a fairly high proportion of sugar, so it's not a pudding to serve regularly. However, it is very high in protein and for a vegetarian child that is a very important factor to bear in mind.

1 Put all but 15 ml (1 tablespoon) of the sugar in a saucepan with the water. Stir over a low heat until all the sugar has dissolved. Increase the heat and bring to the boil. Boil steadily until the mixture turns a deep golden colour.
2 Quickly pour the caramel into the base of six small ramekins or ovenproof teacups. Preheat the oven to Gas Mark 3/170°C/325°F.
3 Whisk the eggs and reserved sugar together. Heat the milk and then whisk it into the eggs. Add the vanilla extract.
4 Strain the mixture into the ramekins or cups and place them in a shallow ovenproof dish. Pour in enough boiling water to come half-way up the sides of the ramekins or cups. Cook for 1 hour, or until the custard is just set and firm to the touch.
5 Remove the ramekins or cups from the dish and leave them to cool. Cover the tops with non-PVC cling film and chill overnight.
6 Using a round-bladed knife, loosen the edges and turn out into serving bowls. Leave upturned in the bowl for several minutes, to allow the caramel to drain out.

Surprise mice

SERVES: *2*
PREPARATION TIME: *10 minutes*
CHILLING TIME: *30 minutes*
FREEZING: *not recommended*

INGREDIENTS
¼-bar of vegetarian lime jelly
150 ml (¼ pint) boiling water
1 pear
6 currants
1 strip of red liquorice bootlace
2 white chocolate buttons, halved
1 small stick of angelica, cut into strips

Getting your children to eat fresh pears couldn't be easier when they are transformed into little mice.

1 Make up the jelly with the boiling water. Add an ice cube and stir until the cube has melted. Pour a layer of jelly on to two serving plates and chill them until set.
2 Peel, core and halve the pear. Place the pear-halves, cored-side down, on each jelly. Arrange the currants for the nose and eyes, liquorice for the tail, buttons for the ears and angelica whiskers.

Easy apple pie

Serves: *4*
Preparation time: *5 minutes*
Cooking time: *20 minutes*
Freezing: *not recommended*

Filo pastry contains very little fat, requires no rolling and can be kept in the freezer. It isn't difficult to handle and makes a delicious, crisp topping for fruit pies.

Ingredients

4 dessert apples, peeled, cored and diced
5 ml (1 teaspoon) caster sugar
2.5 ml (½ teaspoon) ground cinnamon
115 ml (4 fl oz) apple juice
6 sheets of filo pastry
30 g (1 oz) butter or margarine, melted
30 g (1 oz) demerara sugar

1 Preheat the oven to Gas Mark 6/200°C/400°F. Put the apples, caster sugar, cinnamon and apple juice into a saucepan. Cook gently until the sugar has dissolved. Increase the heat and cook, stirring frequently, until the apples are soft.
2 Spoon into four individual pie dishes. Halve two sheets of filo pastry. Scrunch up one half with a whole sheet and lay them on top of the apples. Brush it with the butter and then sprinkle with sugar. Repeat with the remaining filo sheets.
3 Cook for 10–15 minutes, or until the topping is crisp and golden. Serve hot or cold.

Teeny trifles

Serves: *4*
Preparation time: *10 minutes*
Freezing: *not recommended*

Trifles are perennial favourites for "afters", and this one could hardly be easier to prepare.

Ingredients

4 slices of raspberry swiss roll
60 g (2 oz) fresh or frozen raspberries
2 mandarin oranges, peeled and segmented
60 ml (4 tablespoons) fresh orange juice
two 125 g cartons of vanilla yogurt
60 ml (4 tablespoons) fromage frais or crème fraîche
chocolate strands or hundreds and thousands, to decorate

1 Put a slice of swiss roll into the base of four small sundae dishes. Divide the fruit between the dishes and then pour over the orange juice. Leave to soak for 5 minutes and then spoon over the vanilla yogurt to cover the fruit completely.
2 Top with a dollop of fromage frais or crème fraîche and sprinkle with chocolate strands or hundreds and thousands before serving.

18
MONTHS ONWARDS

TEATIME SAVOURIES

A great selection of fun food that will tempt even the fussiest of eaters, from savoury toast-toppers to make-ahead, savoury bakes.

Treasure chests

MAKES: *4*
PREPARATION TIME: *30 minutes*
CHILLING TIME: *15 minutes*
COOKING TIME: *35 minutes*
FREEZING: *recommended, for unfilled treasure chests*

INGREDIENTS
225 g (8 oz) puff pastry
beaten egg to glaze
5 ml (1 teaspoon) sesame seeds
10 ml (2 teaspoons) soft margarine
10 ml (2 teaspoons) unbleached plain flour
150 ml (¼ pint) milk
30 g (1 oz) red Leicester cheese, grated
15 ml (1 tablespoon) smooth peanut butter
30 ml (2 tablespoons) frozen special mixed vegetables
60 g (2 oz) sweetcorn, thawed

You can fill the little puff-pastry cases with whatever your child finds most appealing. I find this a great recipe for using up leftover vegetables which are transformed by the nutty, cheesy sauce.

1 Roll out the pastry to about 2.5 mm (⅛ inch), thick. Cut out four rectangles measuring 8 × 2.5 cm (3 × 1 inch). Place them, spaced a little apart, on a baking sheet. Re-roll the trimmings and cut out four lids. Place them on the baking sheet.
2 Using a small, sharp knife, make a chevron pattern on the lids. Then, taking care not to cut right through, mark a border 5 mm (¼ inch) from the edge of each rectangle. Chill for 15 minutes.
3 Meanwhile, preheat the oven to Gas Mark 7/220°C/425°F. Brush the lids and the borders with egg and bake for 10 minutes, or until they are well risen and golden. Carefully press the centre of each treasure chest to create a cavity.
4 Melt the margarine in a small pan and stir in the flour. Gradually add the milk and stir over a medium heat until thickened. Stir in the cheese, peanut butter and special mixed vegetables. Spoon the filling into the treasure chests, spoon a little sweetcorn for "gold" on top and then put on the lids. Put on serving plates and spoon the remaining "gold" around each.

Sandwich snails

These cute sandwiches can be made with a variety of fillings. For best results, use one that will spread easily.

1 Remove the crusts from the bread. Place the bread on a board, overlapping the ends slightly, and then roll them together with a rolling pin, to seal the ends and flatten the slices.
2 Mix together the cream cheese, mayonnaise, sweetcorn and pepper. Spread over the bread to cover it completely. Starting at a narrower end, roll up the bread like a swiss roll.
3 Slice in half to create two smaller rolls.
4 Place a carrot-half, rounded-side up, on each plate, and position a sandwich on top. Cut four antennae and two mouths from a piece of cucumber. Fix the antennae and mouths in place. Arrange the lettuce around the base of the snail, for grass.

MAKES: *2 snails*
PREPARATION TIME: *10 minutes*
FREEZING: *not recommended*

INGREDIENTS
2 slices of white or wholemeal bread
60 g (2 oz) cream cheese
5 ml (1 teaspoon) mayonnaise
50 g (2 oz) sweetcorn
1 strip of red pepper, cut in tiny cubes
1 long carrot, trimmed, peeled and halved lengthways
cucumber for the antennae and mouth
shredded lettuce for the grass

Moonbeams

Yeast extract contains all the B vitamins, as well as giving good old "eggy bread" a taste lift. Serve with wedges of apple.

1 Remove the crusts from the bread. Using a biscuit cutter, cut out half-moon shapes and spread each with yeast extract.
2 Beat the egg and milk together on a plate. Dip the moonbeams in the egg mixture to coat them. Meanwhile, melt the margarine in a non-stick frying-pan. Fry the moonbeams over a medium heat for 2–3 minutes on each side, until golden.

SERVES: *1*
PREPARATION TIME: *5 minutes*
COOKING TIME: *5 minutes*
FREEZING: *not recommended*

INGREDIENTS
2 slices of white or wholemeal bread
1.25 ml (1/4 teaspoon) yeast extract
1 size-3 egg
45 ml (3 tablespoons) milk
5 ml (1 teaspoon) margarine

HINTS AND TIPS

For a sweet version, use fruit spread in place of yeast extract. If you haven't a cutter, use a small sharp knife and cut the moonbeams freehand.

Fun fingers

MAKES: *4 fingers*
STANDING TIME: *30 minutes*
PREPARATION TIME: *20 minutes*
COOKING TIME: *10 minutes*
FREEZING: *not recommended*

INGREDIENTS
180 g (6 oz) tofu in one piece
20 ml (4 teaspoons) low-sodium light soy sauce
2.5 ml (1/2 teaspoon) sesame oil
1 size-3 egg
85 g (3 oz) white breadcrumbs
15 ml (1 tablespoon) sesame seeds
corn oil for shallow-frying

As tofu has such a bland flavour, it will absorb other tastes quite readily. Serve these fingers with canned spaghetti hoops in tomato sauce and Rösti Potatoes (see page 95).

1 Cut the tofu into equal-sized fingers and put them in a shallow dish. Mix together the soy sauce and sesame oil and pour them over the tofu. Leave to soak for about 30 minutes.
2 Beat the egg on a plate. On a second plate, mix together the breadcrumbs and sesame seeds. Dip the tofu fingers in the egg first and then coat them in the breadcrumbs and sesame seeds.
3 Heat a little oil in a non-stick frying-pan and, turning the fingers, cook them for 4–5 minutes on each side, or until the coating is crisp and golden.

Crumpet clock

SERVES: *1*
PREPARATION TIME: *15 minutes*
COOKING TIME: *5 minutes*
FREEZING: *recommended*

INGREDIENTS
1 crumpet, toasted
10 ml (2 teaspoons) tomato ketchup
1/4 small green pepper, de-seeded
1/2 small yellow pepper, de-seeded
15 g (1/2 oz) slice of red Leicester cheese
2 slices of tiny button mushrooms

You can use crumpets, half a toasted muffin or a bap for these pizza-like snacks.

1 Preheat the grill to high. Spread the crumpet with tomato ketchup to cover it completely. Using a small number-cutter, stamp out 12, 3, 6 and 9 from the green pepper. Then stamp out 1, 2, 4, 5, 7, 8, 10 and 11 from the yellow pepper. Position on the crumpet.
2 Using a sharp knife, cut clock "hands" from the cheese and place on the pizza. Fix the mushrooms at the end of the "hands". Preheat the grill to hot.
3 Brush the vegetables with a little oil and then grill for 5 minutes, or until the cheese is bubbling. Allow to cool slightly before serving.

HINTS AND TIPS
For a party, make a big pizza clock using a 20 cm (8-inch) pizza base.

Smiley clown

This will certainly bring a smile at teatime. The hummus provides the perfect base for the clown's face, plus a fair helping of protein. Serve with breadsticks.

1 On an 18-cm (7-inch) tea plate, spread the hummus in a thin round, using a palette knife if possible.
2 Arrange the features as follows: cherry tomato for the nose, alfalfa sprouts for the hair, hard-boiled egg and crossed strips of green pepper for the eyes and a wedge of cheese for the mouth.
3 Shape a bow tie from the carrot and put it in place.

SERVES: *1*
PREPARATION TIME: *10 minutes*
FREEZING: *not recommended*

INGREDIENTS
30 ml (2 tablespoons) hummus
½ cherry tomato
alfalfa sprouts
2 slices of hard-boiled egg
4 matchstick strips of green pepper
a small wedge of Edam cheese
1 long slice of carrot

Double deckers

Club sandwiches make quite a meal, and can be filled with whatever you have to hand in the fridge. Remember to remove the cocktail sticks before giving these to small children.

1 Spread one slice of bread with peanut butter and the other with cream cheese. Arrange the lettuce, cucumber and tomato on top of one slice and then sandwich the first slice of bread together with the second slice.
2 Cut the sandwich into triangles. Stand the triangles upright on a plate and fix them together with cocktail sticks.

SERVES: *1*
PREPARATION TIME: *10 minutes*
FREEZING: *not recommended*

INGREDIENTS
2 slices of white or wholemeal bread
5 ml (1 teaspoon) smooth peanut butter
15 ml (1 tablespoon) cream cheese
2 frilly lettuce leaves
5 slices of cucumber
1 tomato, thinly sliced

Spotty dogs

The vegetarian hot dog couldn't be simpler. Use a quantity of home-baked beans and ready-made vegetarian sausages for a filling and fast tea.

1 Cook the sausages until golden and cooked through. Meanwhile, heat the beans.
2 Split the roll in half down the centre and spoon in the beans. Place the sausages on top and top with the tomato ketchup. Cut in half crossways to serve.

SERVES: *1*
PREPARATION TIME: *5 minutes*
COOKING TIME: *10 minutes*
FREEZING: *not recommended*

INGREDIENTS
2 vegetarian sausages
1 quantity Home-baked Beans (see page 98)
1 white or wholemeal bridge roll
5 ml (1 teaspoon) tomato ketchup

Scorched corn cobs

SERVES: *1*
PREPARATION TIME: *5 minutes*
COOKING TIME: *12 minutes*
FREEZING: *not recommended*

INGREDIENTS
1 corn on the cob
5 ml (1 teaspoon) butter or margarine, melted
2.5 ml (½ teaspoon) maple syrup

These can be cooked under the grill or on a barbecue. Serve with crusty bread and tomato wedges.

1 Preheat the grill to high. Remove the outer husks and the silk threads from the corn cob. Brush with the melted butter or margarine and the maple syrup.
2 Cook under the grill, turning occasionally and brushing the cob with the melted mixture until the corn kernels turn a deep golden colour. Allow to cool slightly before serving.

Rarebit squares

SERVES: *2*
PREPARATION TIME: *5 minutes*
COOKING TIME: *5 minutes*
FREEZING: *recommended*

INGREDIENTS
60 g (2 oz) Cheddar cheese, grated
1 small apple, grated
5 ml (1 teaspoon) chutney
2 slices of wholemeal bread, toasted

A de luxe version of ordinary cheese on toast. The grated apple adds vitamins and fibre as well as flavour.

1 Preheat the grill to high. Mix together the cheese, apple and chutney. Spread an equal amount over each slice of toast to cover it completely.
2 Grill for 5 minutes, or until the topping is golden and bubbling.

HINTS AND TIPS
Make a larger quantity of the cheesy paste than you need and store the extra in single-portion sizes in the freezer. Unfrozen paste will keep for up to 2 days.

Noughts and crosses

SERVES: *2*
PREPARATION TIME: *5 minutes*
COOKING TIME: *3–4 minutes*
FREEZING: *not recommended*

Use any mild-flavoured cheese that melts easily for this recipe. There is no need to butter the toast, because the cheese will provide enough fat. This is a fun tea for your youngster to enjoy with a friend.

INGREDIENTS
2 slices of wholemeal bread, toasted
8 thin slices of mozzarella cheese
8 cooked green beans
4 cherry tomatoes
4 thin matchstick strips of yellow pepper

1 Preheat the grill to high. Arrange the cheese on the toast to cover it completely. Arrange the beans in a grid on top. Halve the tomatoes and position them on top for noughts. Cut the pepper strips into equal lengths and arrange them on the grid for crosses.
2 Grill for 3–4 minutes, or until the cheese has melted and is bubbling. Allow to cool a little before serving.

Mexican beans

SERVES: *1*
PREPARATION TIME: *10 minutes*
COOKING TIME: *5 minutes*
FREEZING: *not recommended*

Use a portion of home-made baked beans or a selection of canned beans for this.

INGREDIENTS
1 portion Home-baked Beans (see page 98)
30 g (1 oz) sweetcorn
1 strip of green pepper, de-seeded and diced
5 ml (1 teaspoon) tomato ketchup
a pinch of ground cumin
3 cheese nachos
30 g (1 oz) Cheddar cheese, grated

1 Put the beans in a saucepan, with the sweetcorn, pepper, tomato ketchup and cumin. Heat gently until the vegetables are tender.
2 Put the nachos on a plate and pile the bean mixture on to each. Sprinkle with the cheese and serve immediately.

TEATIME BAKES

Make these as treats, rather than serving them every day. During the week, fresh fruit or yogurt should satisfy even the heartiest of appetites.

Frosted carrot cakes

MAKES: *16 cakes*
PREPARATION TIME: *30 minutes*
COOKING TIME: *45 minutes*
FREEZING: *recommended*

INGREDIENTS
115 g (4 oz) soft margarine
115 g (4 oz) light soft brown sugar
115 g (4 oz) self-raising wholemeal flour
2.5 ml (½ teaspoon) baking powder
2.5 ml (½ teaspoon) ground cinnamon
2 size-3 eggs
180 g (6 oz) carrots, grated
grated zest and juice of 1 small unwaxed orange
FOR THE TOPPING:
85 g (3 oz) cream cheese
45 g (1½ oz) icing sugar

HINTS AND TIPS
For children over five years' old, scatter finely chopped walnuts over the top.

Carrot cake is a favourite with all ages. Carrots make a really moist cake and sweeten it, so you don't need so much sugar.

1 Preheat the oven to Gas Mark 4/180°C/350°F. Grease and line the base of a 20-cm (8-inch), shallow, square cake tin. Cream the margarine and sugar until they are pale and fluffy. Sift the flour, baking powder and cinnamon together.

2 Beat the eggs into the creamed mixture and then fold in the flour and carrots. Stir in all but 2.5 ml (½ teaspoon) of the grated orange zest and all the juice. Spoon the cake batter into a tin and level the surface with the back of a spoon. Bake for 45 minutes, or until the cake is well risen and golden, and a skewer comes out clean when you insert it in the centre. Leave to cool on a wire rack.

3 To make the topping, cream together the cream cheese and the icing sugar until the mixture is fluffy. Stir in the reserved orange zest. Spread the topping over the top of the cake and then cut the cake into squares.

Lemon ladies and men

I tend to use a basic shortbread rather than a gingerbread mix for these biscuits, as it produces a much nicer, more crumbly texture, which children seem to prefer.

MAKES: *about 12 people*
PREPARATION TIME: *10 minutes*
CHILLING TIME: *30 minutes*
COOKING TIME: *15–20 minutes*
FREEZING: *recommended*

INGREDIENTS
115 g (4 oz) butter or margarine
60 g (2 oz) caster sugar
grated zest of 1 small unwaxed lemon
115 g (4 oz) unbleached plain flour
60 g (2 oz) cornflour
raisins or currants, to decorate

1 Lightly grease two baking sheets. Cream together the butter and sugar until pale. Stir in the lemon zest and the flours and mix to form a stiff dough. Knead lightly.
2 Roll out the dough on a lightly floured surface and, using gingerbread man and woman cutters, cut out the shapes. Place them, spaced a little apart, on baking sheets. Fix the raisins or currants for eyes and buttons. Mark a mouth with the tip of a knife.
3 Chill for 30 minutes. Meanwhile, preheat the oven to Gas Mark 4/180°C/350°F. Bake the biscuits for 15 minutes, or until golden. Leave to cool slightly on the baking sheet and then transfer them to a wire rack. Store for up to 1 week in an airtight tin.

Date bars

These do not contain processed sugar; all the sweetness is provided by the dates. For a special occasion, top the bars with 60 g (2 oz) of melted chocolate or carob before you cut them.

MAKES: *16 bars*
PREPARATION TIME: *10 minutes*
COOKING TIME: *30 minutes*
FREEZING: *recommended*

INGREDIENTS
225 g (8 oz) block of dates, rinsed, dried and coarsely chopped
150 ml (1/4 pint) unsweetened apple juice
60 g (2 oz) ground walnuts
115 g (4 oz) soft margarine
115 g (4 oz) plain wholemeal flour
60 g (2 oz) porridge oats
1 size-3 egg

1 Preheat the oven to Gas Mark 4/180°C/350°F. Grease an 18 cm (7-inch) shallow square tin. Put the dates and apple juice into a saucepan and bring the juice to the boil. Reduce the heat, cover the pan and let it simmer for 5 minutes.
2 Remove the pan from the heat and leave the dates to cool slightly. Stir in the remaining ingredients and mix well. Spoon them into the tin and level the surface with the back of a spoon. Cook for 30 minutes, or until the mixture is beginning to shrink from the sides of the tin.
3 Allow to cool in the tin for a few minutes. Then turn out and leave to cool on a wire rack. Cut into bars when cooled.

18
MONTHS ONWARDS

PARTY FOOD

A birthday party means treats; this section provides the right balance between "healthy" and indulgent dishes. For toddlers' birthdays keep the food to just three or four dishes. Under the age of four, most children will be more concerned with presents and games than with food, and, remember, it is a day you all *want to enjoy, so don't make life more difficult for yourself than you need.*

Birthday people

MAKES: *8 people*
PREPARATION TIME: *20 minutes*
FREEZING: *not recommended*

INGREDIENTS
4 thin slices of unbleached white or wholemeal bread
a little margarine for spreading
4 thin slices of Cheddar or red Leicester cheese
red and green pepper, carrot, and cress for decoration

This recipe makes eight of these little open sandwiches but be sure to make enough for every party guest.

1 Using a small gingerbread-man and -woman cutter, stamp out four of each from the bread. Spread with margarine. Using the cutter as a guide, cut out shirts and trousers for the men and dresses for the ladies from the cheese. Put the clothes in place.
2 For the men, use strips of carrot for braces and belts and a little green pepper for bow ties.
3 Use red pepper to shape zig-zag (frilly) collars and cuffs for the ladies. Put the sandwiches on a serving plate and attach cress for eyes and nose, and red pepper for mouths.

HINTS AND TIPS
Cover with non-PVC cling film to prevent the people from drying out.

Sesame snaps

These are very moreish and can be cut out in fun shapes or rounds.

Makes: *about 20 biscuits*
Preparation time: *10 minutes*
Chilling time: *15 minutes*
Cooking time: *15 minutes*
Freezing: *recommended*

Ingredients
180 g (6 oz) wholemeal flour
115 g (4 oz) butter or block margarine
2.5 ml (½ teaspoon) yeast extract
15 ml (1 tablespoon) sesame seeds, toasted
60 g (2 oz) Cheddar cheese, grated

1 Lightly grease two baking sheets with oil. Rub the butter into the flour until the mixture resembles fine crumbs. Stir in the yeast extract, 10 ml (2 teaspoons) of the sesame seeds and the cheese. Knead together to form a soft dough.
2 Roll out on a lightly floured surface and stamp out shapes with your chosen cutter. Put the shapes on a baking sheet, spaced a little apart, and prick them with a fork. Sprinkle them with the remaining sesame seeds and chill for 15 minutes.
3 Preheat the oven to Gas Mark 4/180°C/350°F. Cook the sesame snaps for 15 minutes, or until firm. Let them cool on the baking sheet for a few minutes and then transfer them to a wire rack. Once cold, store in an airtight tin for up to a week.

Apple chips

A novel and much healthier version of much-loved crisps.

Serves: *8*
Preparation time: *20 minutes*
Cooking time: *10 minutes*
Freezing: *not recommended*

Ingredients
450 g (1 lb) firm dessert apples
groundnut oil for frying
15 ml (1 tablespoon) caster sugar (optional)

1 Peel, core and quarter the apples. Cut each quarter into very thin slices. Do not rinse.
2 Meanwhile, heat the oil in a deep frying-pan until the temperature reaches 190°C/375°F, or when a cube of bread rises and sizzles within 30 seconds. Cook the apple slices in four batches for 3–4 minutes, or until the apples are crisp and golden.
3 Drain on kitchen paper and sprinkle with a little caster sugar, if you like.

Hints and tips
Caster sugar mixed with a little ground cinnamon is a tasty alternative to sugar only.

Basic birthday cake

PREPARATION TIME: *15 minutes*
COOKING TIME: *according to size of tin*
FREEZING: *recommended*

INGREDIENTS

For every 600 ml (1 pint):

60 g (2 oz) soft margarine
60 g (2 oz) caster sugar
1 size-3 egg
60 g (2 oz) self-raising unbleached flour

A simple, all-in-one cake mixture that you can adapt to suit any size or shape of cake tin. To calculate the amount of cake batter needed for your cake tin, fill the tin with water to the depth you want the cake to be (not right to the top of the tin). For every 600 ml (1 pint) the tin holds, allow the following quantities and multiply them as required.

1 Preheat the oven to Gas Mark 4/180°C/350°F. Grease the tin and line the base with greaseproof paper. Put all the ingredients into a bowl, and, using an electric whisk, beat them until smooth.

2 Spoon the mixture into the tin, level the surface with the back of a spoon and bake for the required time. As a guide, a 4-egg mixture made in two 20 cm (8-inch) sandwich tins will take about 35 minutes. It is difficult to give accurate timings for oddly shaped cakes, such as numerals or novelty tins, because the more contact the mixture has with the sides of the tin, the faster it will cook. Don't use this mixture for cake tins more than 25 cm (10 inches) at their widest point, or the edges will overcook long before the middle is ready.

FLAVOURINGS

Lemon or Orange cake
Use unwaxed fruit and add the grated zest of 1 fruit to the cake batter.

Chocolate or Carob cake
Replace 30 g (1 oz) of the flour with the same amount of cocoa or carob powder.

Marble cake
Put half the cake mixture into a clean bowl and colour one half as desired, using vegetable food colouring paste. Place alternate spoonfuls of plain and coloured batter in the tin, and swirl them gently together with a skewer.

Vanilla buttercream

This can be made with butter or margarine and is perhaps the simplest of fillings or icings for a cake. For more elaborate decorations, it can be piped as well.

Cream the butter or margarine until pale. Gradually beat in the icing sugar, water and vanilla extract. Cover and chill until required. Allow to soften at room temperature before using.

FLAVOURINGS

Chocolate or Carob buttercream
Dissolve 15 ml (1 tablespoon) cocoa or carob powder in 10 ml (2 teaspoons) hot water and then stir the mixture into the buttercream.

Orange or Lemon buttercream
Replace the vanilla extract with the grated zest from 1 unwaxed fruit.

MAKES: *enough to fill and coat the top of a 20 cm (8-inch) cake*
PREPARATION TIME: *10 minutes*
FREEZING: *not recommended*

INGREDIENTS
180 g (6 oz) softened butter or margarine
340 g (12 oz) icing sugar, sifted
15 ml (1 tablespoon) hot water
5 ml (1 teaspoon) vanilla extract

Fondant icing

This is not too tricky to make and easy enough for even the novice in cake decorating to produce an attractive effect. If you can roll out pastry, you can ice a cake with this icing. There are some excellent brands of fondant available today, but here is a recipe for home-made fondant. You'll find liquid glucose in a jar at a good chemist's shop.

1 Sift the icing sugar twice. Put the liquid glucose, egg white and rose-water into a large bowl. Gradually stir in the icing sugar. When the icing is too stiff to stir, knead in the remaining icing sugar by hand until the icing is completely smooth.
2 Knead until the mixture forms a soft ball. Add more icing sugar if the icing remains sticky. Wrap in non-PVC cling film and place in a polythene bag. Store in the fridge.

MAKES: *450 g (1 lb)*
PREPARATION TIME: *10 minutes*
FREEZING: *recommended*

INGREDIENTS
450 g (1 lb) icing sugar
18 ml (1 rounded tablespoon) liquid glucose
1 size-3 egg white
5 ml (1 teaspoon) rose-water

HINTS AND TIPS
Keep the fondant tightly covered, or it will dry out quickly and crack.

SERVES: *8*
PREPARATION TIME: *30 minutes*
FREEZING: *not recommended*

INGREDIENTS
4 ripe avocados
30 ml (2 tablespoons) lemon juice
180 g (6 oz) cream cheese
15 ml (1 tablespoon) mayonnaise
cauliflower florets, cucumber sticks and shapes, multi-coloured peppers, breadsticks and crackers, to serve

Birthday lagoon

A simple avocado dip is transformed into a stunning centrepiece that requires hardly any effort to make.

1 Using a triple thickness of non-aluminium foil, shape a 30 cm (12-inch) shallow lagoon, and place it on a tray or a flat plate larger than the lagoon.
2 Halve each avocado and remove the stones. Scoop the flesh into a bowl and mash it with the lemon juice, cream cheese and mayonnaise, until smooth. Spoon into the lagoon, and, using a fork, spread the dip to form "waves".
3 Arrange the vegetables around the lagoon to resemble trees and flowers. Use the breadsticks and crackers for rocks. Serve immediately.

MAKES: *12 crackles*
PREPARATION TIME: *10 minutes*
COOKING TIME: *5 minutes*
CHILLING TIME: *1 hour*
FREEZING: *not recommended*

INGREDIENTS
225 g (8 oz) Caramac, broken into squares
15 ml (1 tablespoon) golden syrup
60 g (2 oz) butter or margarine
60 g (2 oz) red glacé cherries, chopped
60 g (2 oz) cornflakes, roughly crushed

No-bake cherry crackles

You don't even have to put the oven on for these, and as they are so simple you may like to get the little ones to help.

1 Set 12 paper cake cases on a baking sheet. Melt the Caramac, syrup and butter or margarine together, in a bowl set over a pan of simmering water.
2 Stir in the cherries and cornflakes, and then divide the mixture equally between the paper cases. Chill until set.

Orange boats

A party wouldn't be a proper party without jelly, so make your own with natural fruit juice, a vegetarian setting agent like Gelozone and only a little sugar.

MAKES: *8 boats*
PREPARATION TIME: *30 minutes*
CHILLING TIME: *at least 2 hours*
FREEZING: *not recommended*

INGREDIENTS
4 oranges
10 ml (2 teaspoons) caster sugar
7.5 ml (1½ teaspoons) Gelozone
8 scoops of Home-made Vanilla Ice Cream (see page 119)
4 ice-cream wafers, halved diagonally

1 Halve each orange, and, using a teaspoon, scoop out the flesh. Take care not to pierce the skin. Wash each orange shell and reserve it. Press the flesh through a sieve and collect the juice in a jug. Make up to 600 ml (1 pint) with orange juice.
2 Pour the orange juice into a saucepan and add the sugar. Sprinkle in the Gelozone and then stir over a low heat until dissolved. Leave to cool slightly.
3 Place the orange shells on a baking sheet and pour in the jelly. Chill until completely set. Put on a serving plate and place a scoop of ice cream on top. Fix a wafer "sail" in place before serving.

Traffic-light lollies

Ice lollies are a great treat, and perfect food for a summer party, when they can be served outside. Make them with natural fruit juice, at least a day in advance.

MAKES: *8 lollies*
PREPARATION TIME: *20 minutes*
FREEZING TIME: *allow at least 24 hours*

INGREDIENTS
225 ml (8 fl oz) each cranberry and raspberry juice, and orange juice
60 ml (2 fl oz) lime cordial
180 ml (6 fl oz) water
green natural food colouring, if necessary

1 Pour the cranberry and raspberry juice into the bottom of eight 85 ml (3 fl oz) lolly moulds. Freeze until solid. Top with the orange juice and freeze again, until solid.
2 Make up the lime cordial with the water and colour it pale green if necessary. Pour into the moulds and clip a lolly stick in place. Freeze until solid. To unmould the lollies, immerse them in hot water for 10 seconds only.

HINTS AND TIPS
Set a whole fresh strawberry or raspberry in the bottom of the lolly-mould in the red fruit juice.

Popcorn

Serves: *8*
Preparation time: *5 minutes*
Cooking time: *5 minutes*
Freezing: *not recommended*

Ingredients
90 ml (6 tablespoons) corn oil
180 g (6 oz) popping corn
30 ml (4 tablespoons) maple or golden syrup

A great low-fat food that children love. Popcorn is ideal for giving away in smart wrappers in guests' party bags.

1 Heat half the oil in a large, deep, heavy-based saucepan. Add half the popping corn to the pan. Cover with a tightly fitting lid, and then shake the pan. Cook over a medium heat for 5 minutes. Shake the pan occasionally as the corn begins to pop.
2 Tip the popcorn into a large bowl and repeat with the remaining oil and corn. Warm the syrup and pour it over the popcorn. Mix well to coat the popcorn evenly.

Cheese buttercups

Makes: *12 buttercups*
Preparation time: *30 minutes*
Cooking time: *20 minutes*
Freezing: *recommended*

Ingredients
12 thin slices of white or wholemeal bread
85 g (3 oz) butter or margarine, melted
2 spring onions, finely chopped
1 strip of green pepper, de-seeded and cut in small cubes
60 g (2 oz) sweetcorn
30 ml (2 tablespoons) unbleached plain flour
300 ml (½ pint) milk
60 g (2 oz) Cheddar cheese, grated

Use butter or margarine to coat these little cups.

1 Preheat the oven to Gas Mark 6/200°C/400°F. Using a 7.5-cm (3-inch) flower cutter or a plain cutter, stamp out 12 shapes from the bread. Brush a 12-section patty tin with melted butter or margarine and then press in the shapes. Brush them well with more melted butter to coat.
2 Cook for 10 minutes, or until crisp and golden. Brush with butter during the cooking time, if some patches appear paler than the rest.
3 Add the vegetables to the remaining melted butter and cook over a medium heat for 5 minutes, or until softened. Add the flour and then gradually stir in the milk. Stir over a medium heat until the sauce is thickened and smooth. Add half the cheese.
4 Divide the mixture between the bread cups and sprinkle the remaining cheese on top. Cook for 5 minutes, or until the cheese has melted. Serve hot or cold.

Hints and tips

Freeze the unfilled bread cups and filling separately.

Home-made vanilla ice cream

This is just what it says, true ice cream, not the synthetic emulsions of fat, sugar, colouring and flavouring that are found in many commercial brands. Serve with puréed strawberries.

Makes: *about 1 litre (2 pints)*
Preparation time: *20 minutes*
Standing time: *1 hour*
Freezing time: *4 hours and then overnight*

Ingredients
600 ml (1 pint) full-cream milk
1 vanilla pod
6 size-3 egg yolks
180 g (6 oz) caster sugar
600 ml (1 pint) fresh whipping cream

1 Put a freezer container into the freezer and set the cabinet to fast-freeze. Heat the milk and vanilla pod until the milk is almost boiling and then remove the pan from the heat and leave the milk to infuse for 1 hour.
2 Beat the egg yolks and sugar together until thick. Remove the vanilla pod from the milk and gradually beat the milk into the egg-yolk mixture. Return the mixture to the pan and stir it over a very low heat until the mixture just coats the back of a wooden spoon. Do not let it boil.
3 Pour the mixture into the chilled container and allow to cool. Seal the lid and freeze for 2 hours, or until the ice cream is just beginning to become mushy.
4 Lightly whip the cream until soft peaks form. Using an electric whisk, beat the frozen custard until smooth. Fold in the cream, seal the lid again and freeze for a further 2 hours as before.
5 Beat with an electric whisk until smooth. Then freeze overnight.

Hints and tips
Allow the ice cream to soften in the fridge for 30 minutes before serving.

Flavourings

Chocolate ice cream
Fold in 180 g (6 oz) of chocolate chips, with the cream.

Fruit ice cream
Purée 340 g (12 oz) of fruit, e.g. strawberry, raspberry, peach, with 30 g (1 oz) of icing sugar and stir the purée into the custard before the first freezing stage.

18
MONTHS ONWARDS

MEALS IN A HURRY

There will always be the occasion when you are expected to feed them and fast, so keep a basic store cupboard of dried pasta, canned beans, soups and sauces; coupled with a few fresh ingredients these will enable you to rustle up a nourishing meal in minutes.

Couscous and orange salad

SERVES: *1*
PREPARATION TIME: *10 minutes*
COOKING TIME: *5 minutes*
FREEZING: *not recommended*

INGREDIENTS
- *30 g (1 oz) couscous*
- *150 ml (1/4 pint) hot vegetable stock*
- *1 small orange, peeled and segmented*
- *30 g (1 oz) sultanas*
- *1 spring onion, trimmed and finely chopped*
- *1/2 celery stick, trimmed and chopped*
- *2 tablespoons (30 ml) French dressing*

HINTS AND TIPS
Older children may like the addition of toasted almonds, to add crunch and protein.

Cracked wheat adds bulk and vitamins to this simple salad. Try using cooked brown rice if you haven't any couscous. Serve with pitta bread.

1 Soak the couscous in the vegetable stock for about 10 minutes until all the liquid is absorbed. Spoon into a heatproof sieve, cover and steam over a pan of simmering water for 10 minutes, or until the couscous grains are tender.
2 Meanwhile, mix together the orange, sultanas, spring onion and celery. Add the couscous and pour the dressing on while the couscous is still warm.

Quick cannelloni

Ground walnuts add protein and flavour, but the flavour may be a little bitter if the walnuts have been stored for some time, so check the packet date before using them.

SERVES: *1*
PREPARATION TIME: *10 minutes*
COOKING TIME: *15 minutes*
FREEZING: *not recommended*

INGREDIENTS
2 cannelloni tubes
115 g (4 oz) curd cheese
30 g (1 oz) ground walnuts
½ garlic clove, crushed
30 ml (2 teaspoons) chopped fresh parsley
grated zest of ½ unwaxed small lemon
½ a 200 g can of chopped tomatoes
2 slices of mozzarella cheese

1 Cook the cannelloni in boiling water for 10 minutes, or until tender. Meanwhile, mix together the curd cheese, ground walnuts, garlic, parsley and lemon zest.
2 Preheat the grill to high. Drain the cannelloni, and, using a spoon or piping bag, fill each tube with the cheese mixture. Put the tubes in a heatproof dish and spoon the tomatoes over the top.
3 Cook under the grill until bubbling. Lay the cheese slices on top and cook for 2–3 minutes, or until melted and starting to turn golden. Make sure your child knows that cooked cheese can be very hot, though.

Spanish omelette

Any combination of vegetables can be called a Spanish omelette. Instantly satisfying, this will feed one, two or four, depending on their appetites. Serve with a salad of wedges of baby gem lettuce and fresh tomatoes.

SERVES: *2*
PREPARATION TIME: *5 minutes*
COOKING TIME: *15 minutes*
FREEZING: *not recommended*

INGREDIENTS
45 ml (3 tablespoons) olive oil
1 large potato, peeled and cut into 1 cm (½-inch) cubes
1 onion, peeled and finely chopped
30 g (1 oz) peas
30 g (1 oz) sweetcorn
½ small red and green pepper, de-seeded and choppped
4 size-3 eggs

1 Heat the oil in a non-stick 18 cm (7-inch) frying-pan. Add the potatoes and onions and cook for 5 minutes over a medium heat. Add the peas, sweetcorn and peppers and cook for 5 minutes. Drain off the excess oil.
2 Beat the eggs with 15 ml (1 tablespoon) water and pour them over the vegetables. Cook over a medium heat for 5 minutes, or until the eggs are set. Preheat the grill to high.
3 Cook the top under the grill for a few minutes, until golden.

HINTS AND TIPS
Other vegetables, such as mushrooms, tomatoes or cooked spinach can be used.

Harlequin macaroni

SERVES: *1*
PREPARATION TIME: *10 minutes*
COOKING TIME: *10 minutes*
FREEZING: *not recommended*

INGREDIENTS
45 g (1½ oz) short-cut macaroni
60 g (2 oz) frozen special mixed vegetables
15 g (½ oz) butter or margarine
15 ml (1 tablespoon) unbleached plain flour
150 ml (¼ pint) milk
30 g (1 oz) red Leicester cheese, grated

The bright colours of the special mixed vegetables – and their neat little square shapes – give this recipe its name. The vegetables also add precious vitamins to the classic and nutritious combination of pasta and cheese sauce.

1 Cook the macaroni in boiling water for 6 minutes. Add the vegetables, return to the boil and cook for 4 minutes, or until the pasta and vegetables are tender.
2 Meanwhile, melt the butter or margarine in a saucepan. Stir in the flour and then gradually add the milk. Stir over a medium heat, until thickened. Drain the pasta and vegetables and stir them into the sauce, with half the cheese.
3 Spoon into a serving bowl and serve with the remaining cheese.

Crunchy cheese salad

SERVES: *1*
PREPARATION TIME: *10 minutes*
COOKING TIME: *5 minutes*
FREEZING: *not recommended*

INGREDIENTS
15 ml (1 tablespoon) olive oil
1 slice of white or brown bread, cubed
1 Little Gem lettuce, trimmed and cut in wedges
1 tomato, cut in wedges
2.5 cm (1-inch) piece of cucumber, halved and thickly sliced
45 g (1½ oz) carrot, grated
45 g (1½ oz) Cheddar cheese, grated

Olive oil has a mild distinct flavour; among many of its wonderful attributes it is low in polyunsaturated fat. The moist centre of grated cheese and carrot, means that dressing is not necessary for this salad.

1 Heat the oil in a non-stick frying-pan. Add the bread and fry it over a medium heat until it's golden and crisp on all sides. Drain on kitchen paper.
2 Arrange the wedges of lettuce and tomato and the cucumber slices alternately around the edge of a serving plate. Put the grated carrot and cheese in the centre and sprinkle the croûtons on top.

Tomato piperade

A colourful egg stew that, like Spanish Omelette, can be adapted to make use of whatever vegetables you have available. Serve with crusty bread or toast to mop up the vegetable juices.

1 Heat the olive oil in a saucepan and cook the onion until golden. De-seed and chop the tomato and pepper strips. Add the garlic, peppers and tomatoes and cook for 15 minutes, until the vegetables have softened to a thick pulp.

2 Beat the eggs and add them to the pan. Stir over a low heat for 5 minutes, or until the eggs are set and creamy.

SERVES: *1*
PREPARATION TIME: *10 minutes*
COOKING TIME: *20 minutes*
FREEZING: *not recommended*

INGREDIENTS
10 ml (2 teaspoons) olive oil
1/4 onion, finely chopped
1/2 garlic clove, crushed
3 strips of pepper
2 tomatoes, skinned
1 size-3 egg

Fasta pasta

This can be cooked in one pan, so saving on time, space and washing up. Serve with herb or garlic bread.

1 Melt the butter or margarine in a saucepan and add the mushrooms and spring onion. Cook over a low heat for 5 minutes. Add the tomatoes and bring to the boil.

2 Stir in the pasta and return to the boil. Simmer for 8–10 minutes, or until the pasta is tender. Spoon into a serving bowl and serve with the grated cheese.

SERVES: *1*
PREPARATION TIME: *5 minutes*
COOKING TIME: *10 minutes*
FREEZING: *not recommended*

INGREDIENTS
5 ml (1 teaspoon) butter or margarine
30 g (1 oz) button mushrooms, wiped and thinly sliced
1 spring onion, trimmed and finely chopped
200 g can of chopped tomatoes with herbs
45 g (1 1/2 oz) small pasta shapes, e.g. bows, quills, spirals, etc.
30 g (1 oz) fresh Parmesan cheese, grated

CHAPTER 4

Family meals

As your child or children grow and learn, family mealtimes can gradually become relaxing and enjoyable occasions for every one. In these busy times, however, sitting down together may be quite a rare event. Nevertheless, good behaviour and table manners should be encouraged from the time your baby is able to sit in the high chair and join you at the dining table. Babies are excellent at mimicry, so the best way for them to learn these social skills is to put them into practice yourself.

Getting children involved

In view of today's busy lifestyle, I have devised the recipes for this final chapter in two sections. The first is for rather special main-course recipes and has been selected with family celebrations in mind. Throughout the year, special events crop up, such as birthdays and anniversaries, or simply that the whole family can manage to eat together at the same time. Children like to be included from a very young age; participating in these events can make them feel very grown-up. At the same time, craftily encourage good eating habits. Whether the meal is to be formal or not, get the children involved wherever practicable. Let them help with designing or writing the invitations, writing the shopping lists, preparing some of the food or helping to set the table. Even the smallest toddler can fold a paper napkin in some fashion. The dishes in this section can be made in advance, so there are no last-minute panics, and there are suggestions for suitable vegetable accompaniments, plus advice on how to adapt them very straightforwardly for the children.

In the second part of the chapter is a selection of recipes that you will probably use more often, for quick Suppers. Very often it is the last meal of the day that causes the most consternation to the cook. With a young family to care for, inspiration as well as energy may well be flagging by the evening, which is why I have designed these recipes so that they can be prepared and cooked with the minimum of effort and be on the table in under half an hour.

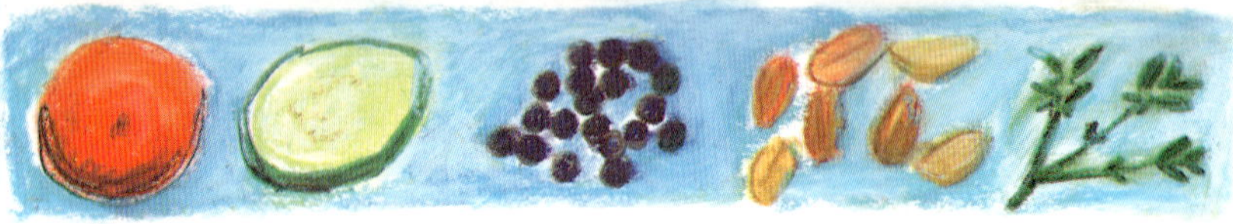

SPECIAL MEALS

Throughout the year, special events crop up that are a cause for celebration: birthdays, anniversaries or simply the whole family managing to be together at the same time. So what better way to do this than with a sumptuous lunch or dinner?

Vegetable terrine

SERVES: *6–8*
PREPARATION TIME: *1¼ hours*
COOKING TIME: *1 hour 20 minutes*
FREEZING: *recommended*

INGREDIENTS
FOR THE FILLING:
600 ml (1 pint) vegetable stock
115 g (4 oz) each brown rice and wild rice
30 ml (2 tablespoons) olive oil
1 onion, finely chopped
1 celery stick, finely chopped
4 carrots, grated
45 ml (3 tablespoons) chopped fresh coriander
3 size-3 eggs, beaten
60 g (2 oz) ground hazelnuts, toasted
10 ml (2 teaspoons) ground cumin
115 g (4 oz) mature Cheddar cheese, grated
freshly ground black pepper
FOR THE HERB CRUST:
180 g (6 oz) each unbleached plain and wholemeal flours
180 g (6 oz) butter or margarine
30 ml (2 tablespoons) chopped herbs
60–75 ml (4–5 tablespoons) milk

This terrine looks spectacular and slices easily. It does require quite lengthy preparation, but this is more than compensated for by the final result. Serve as a main course with stir-fried Brussels sprouts and roasted root vegetables sprinkled with rosemary.

1 Bring the stock to the boil in a large saucepan. Add all the rice and return to the boil. Reduce the heat, cover the pan and leave to simmer for 20 minutes, or until the rice has absorbed most of the stock. Reduce the heat to very low and cook for a further 5 minutes, stirring occasionally.
2 Meanwhile, heat the olive oil in a frying-pan and cook the onion and celery over a medium heat for 5 minutes, or until softened. Add the carrots and cook for 3 minutes more.
3 Stir the vegetables into the rice, with the coriander, two-thirds of the beaten eggs, the hazelnuts, cumin and half the Cheddar cheese. Season with black pepper.
4 Grease and line the base of a 900 g (2 lb) loaf tin measuring 25 × 13 cm (10 × 5 inches). Preheat the oven to Gas Mark 4/180°C/350°F. Spoon the rice mixture into the tin, pressing it down firmly with the back of a spoon. Cook for 50 minutes, or until firm. Leave to cool in the tin.
5 Meanwhile, make the herb crust. Sift the flours into a bowl with a pinch of salt. Rub in the butter or margarine, until the mixture resembles fine breadcrumbs. Stir in the herbs, the remaining Cheddar cheese and enough milk to form a soft, but not sticky, dough. Wrap the dough in non-PVC cling film and chill it until required.

6 Roll out three-quarters of the herb dough on a lightly floured surface to a rectangle large enough to encase the filling. Turn the rice terrine out on to the centre of the pastry and peel away the lining paper. Moisten the edges of the pastry, lift them over the terrine and seal the ends together down the centre of the filling. Tuck in the end flaps and seal them underneath, like a parcel. Put the terrine on a baking sheet.

7 Roll out the reserved pastry and cut out pastry leaves of various sizes. Dampen the leaves and arrange them along the centre of the pastry, to hide the seams. Chill for 15 minutes. Preheat the oven to Gas Mark 6/200°C/400°F.

8 Use the remaining beaten egg to glaze the pastry completely. Bake the terrine for 40 minutes, or until the pastry is golden and the filling thoroughly heated through. Allow to cool for 10 minutes before slicing.

HINTS AND TIPS

Ensure the hazelnuts are finely ground before serving this to children. For a Christmas decoration, use holly-shaped pastry leaves for decorating.

Vegetable satay

SERVES: *6*

PREPARATION TIME: *45 minutes*

STANDING TIME: *30 minutes*

COOKING TIME: *20 minutes*

FREEZING: *not recommended*

INGREDIENTS

1 aubergine, cut in 2.5 cm (1-inch) cubes
10 ml (2 teaspoons) salt
6 corn on the cobs
1 each red, green and yellow pepper, de-seeded and cut in 2.5 cm (1-inch) squares
4 courgettes, cut in 6 pieces
24 cherry tomatoes

FOR THE GLAZE:

45 ml (3 tablespoons) low-sodium soy sauce
15 ml (1 tablespoon) clear honey
15 ml (1 tablespoon) vegetable oil

FOR THE SAUCE:

225 g (8 oz) natural roasted peanuts
60 g (2 oz) butter or margarine
15 ml (1 tablespoon) light muscovado sugar
10 ml (2 teaspoons) tahini paste
1 garlic clove, crushed
250 ml (9 fl oz) water
a pinch each of salt and cayenne pepper

Combined with the vegetables, the peanut sauce essential to satays is a good source of the B vitamins thiamine and niacin, as well as protein and fibre. Serve at a summer barbecue with mushroom kebabs and Lightning Burgers (see page 85).

1 Soak 24 bamboo skewers in hot water. Layer the aubergine cubes in a colander, with the salt. Leave to stand for 30 minutes. Rinse well under cold running water.

2 Remove the husks and silk threads from the corn and cut each in four. Thread all the vegetables and the tomatoes alternately on to the skewers.

3 Warm the soy sauce, honey and oil in a small saucepan and brush the mixture over the kebabs to glaze them. Cook the kebabs on the barbecue or under a preheated grill for 15 minutes, brushing them with the remaining glaze and turning them frequently, until the vegetables are tender.

4 Meanwhile, make the sauce. Chop the peanuts and butter or margarine in a food processor or blender until smooth. Spoon the mixture into a saucepan and stir in the sugar, tahini paste, water, salt and cayenne pepper. Stir over a low heat for 5 minutes, or until the sauce is hot and well amalgamated.

HINTS AND TIPS

Remove the wooden kebab sticks before serving this to children. Make the sauce in advance and store it in a sealed container in the fridge.

Tomato and onion tart

Ideal for a spring lunch party, this is somewhat similar to a pizza, but the pastry shell gives it a lighter texture. To eat it at its best, serve it as soon as it comes out of the oven. Potato salad and a selection of salad leaves are good accompaniments.

SERVES: *6*
PREPARATION TIME: *30 minutes*
CHILLING TIME: *15 minutes*
COOKING TIME: *1 hour*
FREEZING: *recommended, for tart case only*

INGREDIENTS

FOR THE TART CASE:

180 g (6 oz) unbleached plain white flour
85 g (3 oz) butter or margarine
5 ml (1 teaspoon) Dijon mustard
1 size-3 egg

FOR THE FILLING:

900 g (2 lb) onions, thinly sliced
2 garlic cloves, crushed
90 ml (6 tablespoons) olive oil
397 g (14 oz) can of tomatoes
15 ml (1 tablespoon) tomato purée
5 ml (1 teaspoon) sugar
5 ml (1 teaspoon) dried oregano
1 green pepper, de-seeded and cut in strips
60 g (2 oz) each black and green olives, stoned
salt and freshly ground black pepper

1 To make the pastry, sift the flour into a bowl and rub in the butter or margarine, until the mixture resembles fine breadcrumbs. Beat the mustard and egg together and add them to the bowl, with enough water to form a soft, but not sticky, dough.

2 Roll out the dough on a lightly floured surface to about 5 mm (¼ inch) thick and use it to line a 25 cm (10-inch) loose-based flan tin. Prick the base and chill it for 15 minutes.

3 Preheat the oven to Gas Mark 6/200°C/400°F. Line the pastry case with greaseproof paper and baking beans and bake it blind for 10 minutes. Remove the paper and beans and bake for a further 10 minutes, or until the pastry has set and is very pale golden.

4 For the filling, cook the onions and garlic in 75 ml (5 tablespoons) of olive oil over a low heat for 40 minutes, or until the onions are soft and pale golden.

5 Meanwhile, put the tomatoes, tomato purée, sugar and oregano into a clean saucepan and bring to the boil. Boil steadily, stirring occasionally until the mixture is reduced to about 6 tablespoons. Stir the tomato mixture into the onions and season well with salt and pepper.

6 Spoon the mixture into the pastry case and level the surface with the back of a spoon. Arrange the pepper strips in a lattice pattern on top and place the olives in alternate spaces. Brush the top with some of the remaining olive oil and bake for 10 minutes.

7 Brush the top with oil again and bake for further 10 minutes, or until the peppers have softened.

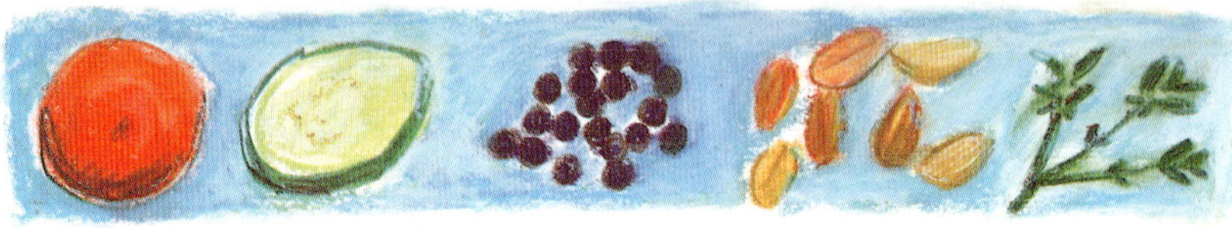

Corn jambalaya

SERVES: *6*
PREPARATION TIME: *20 minutes*
COOKING TIME: *30 minutes*
FREEZING: *not recommended*

INGREDIENTS

90 ml (6 tablespoons) groundnut oil
15 ml (1 tablespoon) granulated sugar
6 corn on the cobs
1 each red and green pepper, de-seeded and chopped
2 celery sticks, thickly sliced
1 onion, chopped
1 garlic clove, crushed
180 g (6 oz) long-grain brown rice
400 ml (¾ pint) vegetable stock
450 g (1 lb) tomatoes; skinned, de-seeded and chopped
2.5 ml (½ teaspoon) dried thyme
a pinch of ground allspice
1 pinch of cayenne pepper
400 g can of gunga peas, drained and rinsed
30 ml (2 tablespoons) chopped fresh parsley
30 g (1 oz) flaked almonds, toasted

For an autumn supper party, a hearty rice stew that really needs no other dish to accompany it, except perhaps some corn muffins and steamed broccoli. The caramelized corn takes only a few minutes; keep watching the pan, or the corn will quickly burn. Gunga peas are like small, round borlotti beans; they are available in good ethnic grocers.

1 Heat the oil and sugar together over a low heat until the sugar has dissolved. Increase the heat and cook until the sugar is a light caramel. Meanwhile, remove the outer husks and silk threads from the corn cobs. Cut each in four pieces.

2 Add the corn cobs to the pan and cook them over a low heat for about 8 minutes, turning them frequently to coat them evenly in the caramel mixture. Remove the pan from the heat, and, using a slotted spoon, lift the corn cobs out. (You may have to cook the cobs in batches.)

3 Add the peppers, celery, onion and garlic to the pan. Return the pan to the heat and cook, stirring occasionally, for 5 minutes, or until the vegetables have softened. Mix in the rice, stock, tomatoes, thyme, spices and peas. Bring to the boil.

4 Reduce the heat, cover the pan and leave to cook gently for 20 minutes.

5 Stir in the corn cobs and cook them for a further 5–10 minutes, or until the rice and vegetables are tender. Sprinkle over the parsley and almonds just before you serve.

HINTS AND TIPS

Provide plenty of napkins so your guests can wipe their sticky fingers after eating the corn cobs.

Quick Suppers

To me, super-quick recipes should be just what the description says: super meals you can prepare and cook in under 30 minutes. No one wants to spend hours cooking during a weekday evening, but you still want to feed your family well. In this section there is over a week's worth of recipes and ideas to enable you to achieve just that.

No-crust quiche

Often the most tricky part of a quiche is the pastry, so why not skip it and cook just the filling? It's a great way to use up cooked, leftover vegetables and pulses; the variations are endless, though here is a popular favourite. Serve with baked beans and crusty bread.

SERVES: *4*
PREPARATION TIME: *10 minutes*
COOKING TIME: *20 minutes*
FREEZING: *not recommended*

INGREDIENTS
15 ml (1 tablespoon) olive oil
1 large onion, finely sliced
1 garlic clove, crushed
180 g (6 oz) Cheddar cheese, grated
3 size-3 eggs, beaten
300 ml (½ pint) single cream
a pinch of grated nutmeg
2 firm tomatoes, sliced
salt and freshly ground black pepper

1 Preheat the oven to Gas mark 5/190°C/375°F. Lightly grease an 18 cm (7-inch) quiche dish. Heat the oil in a small pan and fry the onion and garlic for 5 minutes, until golden. Spoon the onion into the base of the dish and sprinkle the cheese on top.
2 Beat together the eggs, cream and nutmeg. Season well with salt and pepper. Strain the eggs over the cheese mixture in the dish and arrange the tomato slices on top.
3 Bake for 25 minutes, or until the mixture is set and the top golden.

Alpine fondue

SERVES: *4–6*
PREPARATION TIME: *10 minutes*
COOKING TIME: *15 minutes*
FREEZING: *not recommended*

INGREDIENTS
1 garlic clove, crushed
300 ml (½ pint) dry white wine or white grape juice
juice of ½ small lemon
180 g (6 oz) Emmenthal cheese, grated
400 g (14 oz) Gruyère cheese, grated
10 ml (2 teaspoons) cornflour
45 ml (3 tablespoons) water
salt and freshly ground black pepper

A great supper dish to make, even if you don't have a fondue set. It is fairly high in fat, so offset this by providing a selection of raw crunchy vegetables for dipping in. Serve with cubes of crusty bread, cauliflower florets, sliced carrots, button mushrooms, baby corn cobs and de-seeded and chopped sweet peppers.

1 Put the garlic, wine and lemon juice in a large, heavy-based saucepan. Stir in the cheeses. Stir over a low heat until all the cheese has melted.
2 Blend the cornflour with the water, to form a smooth paste. Stir the paste into the melted cheese and cook over a medium heat, until it has thickened and is smooth.
3 Season with salt and pepper and serve at once, dipping the bread and vegetables into the cheese.

HINTS AND TIPS
Children love dipping into fondues, but the cheese can be dangerously hot; for safety, provide younger children with their very own dish of fondue mixture set on a dinner plate.

Country-style eggs

SERVES: *4*
PREPARATION TIME: *20 minutes*
COOKING TIME: *10 minutes*
FREEZING: *not recommended*

This is a meat-free version of the classic recipe for scotch eggs. High in fibre and protein, country-style eggs make a satisfying supper, with coleslaw, steamed corn and tomatoes; or serve them cold in a lunch box.

INGREDIENTS

1 packet of country-style stuffing mix
30 g (1 oz) unbleached plain flour
4 size-3 hard-boiled eggs, shelled
1 size-3 egg
115 g (4 oz) wholemeal breadcrumbs
30 g (1 oz) pumpkin seeds, roughly crushed
corn oil for deep-frying

1 Make up the stuffing with boiling water according to the packet instructions. Divide the mixture into quarters and roll out one quarter on a lightly floured surface, to a 13–15 cm (5–6-inch) round. Dampen the edges and wrap it around a hard-boiled egg, to seal the egg in completely. Repeat with the remaining stuffing and eggs.
2 Beat the egg on a plate, and mix together the breadcrumbs and pumpkin seeds on a second plate. Coat each stuffing-coated egg in egg first, and then in the breadcrumb mixture.
3 Heat the oil in a deep saucepan, until the temperature reaches 190°C/375°F, or when a cube of bread rises and sizzles within 30 seconds. Deep-fry the eggs for 8–10 minutes over a medium-low heat, until they are crisp and golden. Drain them on kitchen paper.

French onion soup

SERVES: *4*
PREPARATION TIME: *5 minutes*
COOKING TIME: *25 minutes*
FREEZING: *not recommended*

A rich, satisfying winter soup that makes the most of simple, storecupboard ingredients. Use sweet yellow or Spanish onions, if they're available.

INGREDIENTS

60 g (2 oz) butter or margarine
2 onions, sliced
2.5 ml (½ teaspoon) dark muscovado sugar
30 ml (2 tablespoons) unbleached plain flour
900 ml (1½ pints) vegetable stock
1 bay leaf
salt and freshly ground black pepper
TO SERVE:
4 slices of French bread
85 g (3 oz) Gruyère, Cheddar or red Leicester cheese, grated

1 Melt the butter or margarine in a saucepan. Add the onions and sugar and cook the onions over a medium–high heat, stirring occasionally, for 10 minutes or until they are a deep golden brown.
2 Remove the pan from the heat and stir in the flour. Gradually stir in the stock. Add the bay leaf and season with salt and pepper. Stir the soup over a medium heat until it has thickened slightly. Cover the pan and leave the soup to simmer for about 20 minutes.
3 Meanwhile, toast the bread on one side. Sprinkle the cheese on the untoasted side and grill until the cheese is golden and bubbling. Ladle the soup into bowls and float a slice of bread on top.

Polenta with cheese

SERVES: *4*
PREPARATION TIME: *40 minutes*
COOKING TIME: *20 minutes*
FREEZING: *not recommended*

INGREDIENTS
15 ml (1 tablespoon) olive oil
3 spring onions, chopped
450 g (1 lb) tomatoes, skinned and roughly chopped
15 ml (1 tablespoon) tomato purée
a pinch of dried basil
225 g (8 oz) polenta
85 g (3 oz) crumbly cheese, e.g. Lancashire, Wensleydale or Cheshire
salt and freshly ground black pepper

Polenta or cornmeal is a great source of energy and vitamins. It is high in carbohydrate and cooks to a smooth, creamy porridge, rather like mashed potatoes. Serve this polenta bake with steamed green beans or a mixed-leaf salad.

1 Heat the oil in a saucepan and add the spring onions, tomatoes, tomato purée and basil. Season lightly with salt and pepper and bring to the boil. Allow to simmer over a low heat, uncovered, until the mixture has thickened slightly.
2 Meanwhile, bring 1 litre (2 pints) of unsalted water to the boil. Add the polenta in a slow, steady stream, stirring continuously. Stir the polenta over a low heat, and, as it begins to thicken, beat the polenta until it begins to pull away from the sides of the pan.
3 Quickly spoon the polenta into a lightly oiled, shallow, flameproof dish. Make a well in the centre and pour in the tomato mixture. Crumble the cheese on top of the tomatoes and grill until golden.

Forest-mushroom risotto

SERVES: *4*
PREPARATION TIME: *5 minutes*
COOKING TIME: *25 minutes*
FREEZING: *not recommended*

INGREDIENTS
30 g (1 oz) dried mixed mushrooms, e.g. ceps, chanterelles or morels
30 ml (1 tablespoon) olive oil
1 red onion, sliced
1 garlic clove, crushed
225 g (8 oz) button mushrooms
225 g (8 oz) arborio, risotto or round-grain pudding rice
1 litre (2 pints) vegetable stock
45 ml (3 tablespoons) chopped fresh parsley
salt and freshly ground black pepper
45 g (1½ oz) fresh parmesan cheese, to serve

Dried mushrooms are a great storecupboard standby. Their flavour is more intense than fresh mushrooms, so only a few are needed. Remember to soak them in the morning, ready for supper.

1 Put the mushrooms in a small bowl and pour over enough boiling water to cover them by about 1 cm (½ inch). Leave to soak for at least 30 minutes.
2 Drain the soaked mushrooms and chop them roughly. Heat the oil in a large saucepan and cook the onion and garlic until softened. Stir in all the mushrooms and rice and half the stock. Bring the stock to the boil.
3 Cook the risotto over a medium heat, stirring frequently, until all the stock has been absorbed. Stir in the remaining stock and continue cooking, stirring occasionally, until the rice is tender and all the stock has been absorbed.
4 Stir in the parsley. Season the risotto with salt and pepper and spoon it into warm bowls. Sprinkle over the parmesan cheese just before you serve.

Three-pepper pizza

To save time, use a ready-prepared pizza base or the toasted halves of a ciabatta loaf that has been sliced lengthways; if you've planned ahead, make the pizza base in advance. Serve with cucumber sticks and wedges of Little Gem lettuce.

1 Heat half the oil in a large frying-pan and cook the pepper rings over a medium heat until they are softened. Remove them with a slotted spoon.

2 Heat the remaining oil in the pan and add the onion, garlic, tomatoes and tomato purée and bring to the boil. Reduce the heat and leave to simmer for 5 minutes. Preheat the oven to Gas Mark 6/ 200°C/400°F.

3 Put the pizza base on a baking sheet and spoon the tomato mixture over it. Arrange the pepper rings and mozzarella slices on top and then sprinkle over the oregano. Cook for 20 minutes, or until the cheese is bubbling.

SERVES: *4*
PREPARATION TIME: *10 minutes*
COOKING TIME: *20 minutes*
FREEZING: *not recommended*

INGREDIENTS

30 ml (2 tablespoons) olive oil
1 each red, green and yellow peppers, de-seeded and sliced in rings
1 red onion, sliced
1 garlic clove, crushed
397 g (14 oz) can of chopped tomatoes with herbs
15 ml (1 tablespoon) tomato purée
25 cm (10-inch) pizza base
115 g (4 oz) mozzarella cheese, sliced
2.5 ml (½ teaspoon) dried oregano

HINTS AND TIPS

Make mini-pizzas for children, using muffin halves or crumpets for the base.

Glossary of terms

Glossary

Agar flakes/powder Setting, thickening and gelling agent made from seaweed. Rich in iron and other minerals and has no flavour, so is suitable for sweet and savoury dishes. In Britain, available under the commercial title Gelozone.

Arrowroot powder Derived from the root of the plant. Used to make thin, clear sauces and glazes. In wholefood shops, sometimes sold under the Japanese title "kuzu"

Bean sprouts Sprouting shoots from seeds or pulses: most commonly available type is mung-bean sprouts. Easy to prepare at home.

Blanch Cook briefly in boiling water for a few minutes.

Bulgur Kernels of wheat that have been cooked, dried and cracked. Finely cracked grains require no cooking, only soaking in boiling water or stock. Cook larger grains like rice.

Carob bars/powder Made from roasted, ground seedpods of locust tree. Naturally sweet, it tastes similar to chocolate.

Caramelize Turn sugar into caramel by heating it gently until it turns golden brown. Some vegetables can be caramelized by cooking them in sugar, water and butter to produce a light golden glaze.

Chick-peas Hard, cream-coloured pulse; can be bought dried or canned. Used in salads and stews, or ground to make flour (gram flour). Mashed, is the main ingredient in hummus.

Charlotte Moulded dish set in round tin or ramekin.

Cornmeal Sometimes called maize meal or polenta; finely ground golden grain extracted from whole corn kernels. Cooked polenta is soft and porridge-like, and can be further baked or roasted. Also used in baking.

Creamed coconut Solidified extract of coconut; can be crumbled directly into stews or dissolved in boiling water. Used in both sweet and savoury dishes.

Garam masala Basic ground curry powder.

Glaze Make baked food look glossy or brown by brushing with milk or beaten egg before cooking.

Gluten Protein found in grains such as wheat. When mixed with liquid, produces elasticity in dough and helps it rise.

Hull Remove stalks and core or calyx from soft fruit, such as strawberries.

Kilocalorie Measurement of energy value of foods.

Marinate Soak food in liquid to add flavour and, sometimes, improve tenderness.

Poach Cook food in very gently simmering liquid.

Poppyseeds Tiny black seeds used in salads, baking and as garnish. Good source of protein.

Purée Blend and/or sieve food until smooth.

Reduce Concentrate or thicken liquid by rapid boiling.

Risotto Savoury dish of rice and vegetables.

Sesame seeds Small, pearly, pale seeds add nutty flavour when toasted and used in toppings, coatings, etc. Pungent oil from ground roasted seeds used in Chinese recipes.

Skim Remove froth or scum from surface of boiling liquid.

Soya flour High-protein, gluten-free baking and thickening agent, made from ground soya beans.

Soya milk Soya beans soaked, ground and filtered to produce milk.

Soy sauce Fermented soya beans used as a condiment and flavouring in savoury dishes, especially Chinese and Far-Eastern cooking. Look out for the low-sodium brands and avoid those containing monosodium glutamate, a worthless chemical flavour enhancer.

Stir-fry Fry evenly sized ingredients at high temperature in wok or large frying-pan, stirring continually.

Tahini Sesame seed paste.

Tofu Japanese word for soya-bean curd. Bland, almost tasteless food that looks like soft white cheese and is extremely high in protein. Can be bought as soft and crumbly *silken tofu, firm tofu* and *smoked tofu*, which slices like cheese.

Wholefoods Grains, pulses, seeds, berries, etc. that have not been treated chemically or refined.

Wholemeal Milled flour that still contains the components of the whole grain: bran, germ and gluten.

Yeast Fungus cells used to produce fermentation and cause dough to rise.

Yeast extract Savoury spread or seasoning, fortified with B-group vitamins and folic acid. Liquid from yeast, evaporated and mixed with vegetable extract and salt.

Useful basic recipes

Pasta The subject of pasta could be a book in itself; there are endless varieties and shapes. However, the basic recipe couldn't be easier. A pasta machine helps take the hard work out of rolling the prepared dough.

This recipe makes about 350 g (12 oz).

INGREDIENTS

225 g (8 oz) strong durum wheat flour
2 size 3 eggs
30 ml (2 tablespoons) olive oil
semolina or farina for sprinkling

1 Sift the flour into a bowl. Make a well in the centre. Beat together the eggs and oil then add to the flour. Mix gently to form a soft dough.

2 Knead pasta dough on a lightly floured surface for 5 minutes or until silky smooth. Halve the dough and roll out each piece to a 10 x 33 cm (16 x 13 inch) rectangle. Trim edges, then cut into even sheets for cannelloni or lasagne.

To make pasta strands:

Roll out two rectangles as before. Sprinkle each lightly with semolina, then roll up each piece loosely like a Swiss roll. Using a very sharp knife cut into even strips, immediately unroll strands and place on a baking sheet sprinkled with semolina to prevent sticking.

White pouring sauce (béchamel sauce) Savoury white sauce forms the basis to many dishes. Once you have mastered the basic technique the varieties are endless.

This recipe makes about 600 ml (1 pint).

INGREDIENTS

600 ml (1 pint) milk
1 bouquet garni
pinch fresh grated nutmeg
25 g (1 oz) butter or margarine
25 g (1 oz) plain flour
salt and freshly ground black pepper

1 Put the milk into a saucepan with the bouquet garni and nutmeg. Heat gently until almost boiling, then remove from the heat. Cover and leave to infuse for at least 2 hours.

2 Melt butter in a clean saucepan, then remove from the heat and stir in the flour. Cook over low heat for 1 minute. Strain milk. Remove the pan from the heat and gradually add the milk a little at a time, stirring well between each addition.

3 Stir the sauce over a medium heat for 3–4 minutes or until the sauce thickens and is smooth. Simmer very gently for a further 4–5 minutes, stirring occasionally. Season with salt and pepper.

Variations:

Herb sauce – Stir in 45 ml (3 tablespoons) fresh chopped herbs, e.g. parsley, chervil, sage or chives at step 3.

Cheese sauce – Stir in 50 g (2 oz) grated or crumbled cheese at step 3, with a pinch of dried mustard.

Vegetable stock A good, home-made stock can be the base for a great many vegetarian recipes. Commercial brands are available but beware, they often contain generous quantities of salt and sugar, which are unsuitable for babies. Vegetable stock will keep for up to five days in the refrigerator. If you want to freeze the stock, pour it into ice-cube trays or plastic containers. Use from frozen.

The recipe given here makes about 1 litre (2 pints).

INGREDIENTS

1 small onion
1 carrot
1 celery stick
115 g (4 oz) turnip
115 g (4 oz) parsnip
115 g (4 oz) swede
30 g (1 oz) fresh root ginger
1 sprig of fresh parsley
1 bay leaf
2 cloves
6 black peppercorns
about 1.4 litres (2½ pints) cold water

1 Roughly chop all the vegetables and ginger. Put them in a saucepan, with the herbs and spices. Add the water and bring it slowly to the boil.
2 Cover and pan and leave to simmer gently for about 2 hours, stirring occasionally. Remove from the heat and leave until cold. Strain through a fine sieve and discard the flavourings. Pour the stock into a large jug, cover it and chill until required.

Tomato sauce Commercial brands cannot compete with this delicious homemade variety. Low in fat, salt and sugar, it can be used in a variety of ways. The sauce can be left chunky, and can be frozen for up to 6 months.

This recipe makes 600 ml (1 pint).

INGREDIENTS

15 ml (1 tablespoon) olive oil
1 medium onion, peeled and finely chopped
1 garlic clove, crushed
5 ml (1 teaspoon) each chopped fresh thyme, oregano and parsley
450 g (1 lb) ripe tomatoes, skinned, deseeded and chopped
397 g (14 oz) can Italian peeled tomatoes
freshly ground black pepper

1 Heat the oil in a large saucepan. Add the onion and garlic and cook over a medium heat for 10 minutes, stirring occasionally.
2 Add the herbs, fresh tomatoes, canned tomatoes and their juice. Bring to the boil, reduce heat, partially cover the pan and simmer for 45–50 minutes, stirring occasionally.
3 Season sauce well with pepper, cool slightly then liquidise to a smooth consistency. Store in a sealed container in the fridge for up to 3 days.

Tomato purée Concentrated tomato purée adds flavour and colour to soups and stews. Make this during the summer when fresh tomatoes are at their best, both in quality and price.

This recipe makes about 400 ml (¾ pint).

INGREDIENTS

1.3 kg (3 lb) fresh ripe tomatoes
pinch salt and sugar

1 Wash and roughly chop the tomatoes. Put into a large saucepan and cook over a medium heat until softened. Bring to the boil, reduce heat, cover and simmer for 20 minutes, stirring occasionally.
2 Cool slightly, then purée in a food processor or blender. Pass purée through a nylon sieve into a saucepan to remove pips. Add salt and sugar, then bring purée to the boil, reduce heat and simmer very gently, stirring occasionally, for about 1½–1¾ hours, or until mixture becomes so thick, it will remain in two halves when a wooden spoon is drawn through the centre.
3 Allow mixture to cool then spoon into an airtight container and store in fridge for up to 1 month.

To freeze:
Freeze in ice cube trays, then turn out frozen cubes and store in plastic bags for up to 8 months.

Fruit tea bread Teabreads are usually enriched with fruit and served sliced, spread with butter or margarine. Many places have their own traditional recipe but this is one I make time after time. It is just as good for breakfast or in a packed lunch as it is at tea time. The loaves can be frozen.

This recipe makes 1 loaf.

INGREDIENTS

175 g (6 oz) each sultanas and currants
225 g (8 oz) dark soft brown sugar
1 orange, grated rind and juice
300 ml (½ pint) strong hot tea
275 g (10 oz) self-raising wholemeal flour
1 size 3 egg, beaten

1 Put the fruit into a large bowl and stir in the sugar, orange rind and juice, then pour in the hot tea. Cover and leave to soak overnight.
2 Preheat the oven at Gas Mark 3/150°C/300°F. Grease and line the base of a 900 g (2 lb) loaf tin. Sift the flour into the fruit, adding any bran left in the sieve. Beat in the egg, then spoon mixture into loaf tin. Level the surface and bake for 1½–1¾ hours, or until a skewer inserted into the centre comes out clean.
3 Allow the tea bread to cool in the tin for about 20 minutes, then turn out and cool on a wire rack. Store in an airtight tin.

Wholemeal bread Bread has been one of the main staples of the world for centuries. Most bread is made with yeast; the dough is kneaded, shaped and allowed to rise. Breads that contain no yeast such as naan or ciabatta are called unleavened. Fresh yeast can be bought at independent bakers or health food shops and any not used can be frozen. The bread dough and the cooked loaves can also be frozen.

This recipe makes 2 loaves.

INGREDIENTS

40 g (1½ oz) fresh yeast
900 ml (1½ pints) tepid water
1.4 kg (3 lb) strong wholemeal flour
2 teaspoons (10 ml) caster sugar
4 teaspoons (20 ml) salt
25 g (1 oz) margarine

1 Mix the yeast with about 300 ml (½ pint) of the water until dissolved. Mix the flour, sugar and salt in a large bowl. Rub in the margarine then make a well in the centre and add the yeast and enough of the remaining water to form a soft slightly sticky dough.
2 Knead the dough on a lightly floured surface for 10 minutes or until it is smooth, soft and elastic. Put it in a clean bowl, cover with greased cling film and leave in a warm place for about 1 hour or until dough has doubled in size.
3 Turn out and knead again for 10 minutes. Grease two 900 g (2 lb) loaf tins. Halve the dough and knead each half again until smooth, then shape to fit the tins. Put dough in tins and cover with greased non PVC cling film. Leave in a warm place until dough reduces the top rim of each tin.
4 Set the oven at Gas Mark 8/240°C/450°F. Uncover dough, brush tops with milk and bake in centre of oven for 35–40 minutes or until the base of each loaf sounds hollow when tapped. Cool on a wire rack.
To make rolls: Divide dough into 50 g (2 oz) pieces and shape into rounds, or ovals. Bake for 15–20 minutes.

Beans, pulses, peas and lentils

Beans and pulses All dried beans and most pulses need to be soaked, so they absorb water and return to their natural size. Soaking doubles the weight of dried beans, so when a recipe calls for 225 g (8 oz) of cooked beans you need to soak 115 g (4 oz).

Spread the beans out in a single layer on a plate and discard any discoloured ones or pieces of grit. Rinse the beans in a colander until the water runs clear and then put them in a bowl large enough to allow the beans to expand. There are two methods of soaking: hot-soaking and cold-soaking. Hot-soaking is the quickest: most beans will have absorbed the maximum amount of water within about 2 hours. Cold-soaking needs at least 6 hours and most recipes recommend cold-soaking overnight. Whatever method you choose, pour over enough boiling or cold water to cover the beans by at least 10 cm (4 inches).

Drain the soaked beans and put them in a large saucepan. Cover with fresh, cold water and bring to the boil. Do not add salt; added salt is harmful to youngsters and will toughen the beans. Boil briskly, uncovered, for 10 minutes; this is essential for all beans, to rid them of toxic substances that can upset the digestive system. Reduce heat, partially cover the pan with a lid and leave to simmer for about an hour.

Peas and lentils Whole peas and chick-peas need to be soaked and cooked in the same way as beans and pulses. Split-peas and lentils do not need soaking or pre-cooking: add them to your recipe and cook for 30–40 minutes, or until tender.

To cook them on their own, rather as an ingredient in a recipe, put them in a saucepan and cover them with unsalted water or vegetable stock. Allow about 1.7 litres (3 pints) of liquid for every 115 g (4 oz). Bring the liquid to the boil, skim the surface to remove any froth, and then partially cover the pan and leave to simmer gently for ¾–1 hour for split-peas, 20 minutes for red lentils and 30–35 minutes for green or brown lentils.

Sprouting beans, peas and seeds
Home-sprouting is easily done and doesn't need much equipment or storage space. A wide-necked jam jar, a piece of clean muslin or J-cloth and an elastic band are all you need. Bean sprouts are highly nutritious, being very rich in protein, fibre, vitamins, minerals and starch. Children love growing their own sprouts, and, as the germination time is fairly short (3–6 days, depending on the type) the fruits of their labours can soon be seen.

Use beans that are intended for eating or sprouting and not ones intended for planting, which may have been treated with a preservative. Choose any of the following: aduki beans, chick-peas, lentils, mung beans or soya beans. Soak soya beans for a couple of hours to soften the outer husks. Seeds to try sprouting are alfalfa, poppy, sesame, sunflower or pumpkin seeds, or whole grains such as wheat.

Three steps to sprouting success

1 Soak or rinse the seed or beans and put them in a large, wide-necked jam jar, with 1–2 tablespoons of water. Cover the jar with muslin and secure it with an elastic band. Store out of the light at a constant room temperature.

2 Every day, pour cold water into the jar through the muslin. Drain off excess water, shaking the beans gently as you do so. Leave the jar upside-down for a few minutes, to drain off the last drops of water. Replace out of the light. Don't let the beans sit in water, or they will rot.

3 The bean sprouts are ready for harvesting when the shoots are about 2.5 cm (1 inch) long. Put them in a colander and rinse them well with cold water.

Index

Credits

Quarto would like to thank the following for permission to reproduce copyright material.

p.6: M. Tcherevkoff/Image Bank; p.16: Pictor; p.36: Terry Williams/ Image Bank; p.68: Jeff Robins/Ace; p.70: Mark French/Ace; p.124: Juan Silva/Image Bank.